Smart Start-Ups

Smart Start-Ups

How Entrepreneurs and Corporations
Can Profit by Starting
Online Communities

David Silver

John Wiley & Sons, Inc.

Published by John Wiley & Sons, Inc., Hoboken, New Jersey.
Published simultaneously in Canada.

Wiley Bicentennial Logo: Richard J. Pacifico.

For general information on our other products and services or for technical
support, please contact our Customer Care Department within the United States
at (800) 762-2974, outside the United States at (317) 572-3993 or fax (317) 572-4002.

Wiley also publishes its books in a variety of electronic formats. Some content that
appears in print may not be available in electronic books. For more information about
Wiley products, visit our web site at www.wiley.com.

ISBN 978-0-470-10742-3

Printed in the United States of America.

10 9 8 7 6 5 4 3 2 1

Dayn M. Schulman, in Memoriam

Contents

Preface

I say, beware of all enterprises that require new clothes, and not rather a new wearer of clothes.

—Henry David Thoreau

I HAVE WRITTEN THIS BOOK to encourage the massive and worldwide formation of useful, sustainable and profitable online and mobile phone-based communities. There is no doubt in my mind that online and mobile communities represent the greatest era of new company formation and potential entrepreneurial wealth creation in modern economic history. And the first phase has begun with the hoopla expected when there are attacks on media companies. MySpace, YouTube and Facebook have leapt onto the stage of phenomenally successful new companies, and they're scaring the pants off of old media companies.

But I'm not at all optimistic about the staying power of MySpace and Facebook. YouTube is a form of citizen journalism, and could survive by adopting the business model of OhMyNews.com, the leader in that genre, whose business model I discuss in the book. Other than providing a playground for young people to meet and communicate, I question the economic durability of MySpace and Facebook, which need to segue to a mobile phone–based business model pretty soon, before a newcomer captures that highly lucrative market from them. Their revenues appear to come solely from advertising. But is advertising core to the business of a playground where people meet to communicate? No. Advertising is not core in the world of communities. The owners of these communities make no request for members to purchase something. There is no persuasion to pay a membership fee or to pay for the privilege of sharing; and thus, the members are likely to flee to a more reciprocal community in which they receive a benefit for which they pay. The owners of MySpace were smart to sell, and they got a very good price. The owners of YouTube were three times smarter.

Most of what is needed by a community founder can be learned from studying the great predecessor offline community businesses, and I present descriptions of these earlier giants in this book. There are hundreds of thousands of examples, some of which, like Tupperware, Weight Watchers International and Mary Kay Cosmetics, are still thriving. Tupperware does more than $1 billion in revenues a year using the community business model. What differentiates the new communities from the old model is multiple methods of communications—the Internet and the mobile phone, primarily. A member of an online or mobile community can be actively searching and sharing information, videos, music, stories, photos, news of events and breakthrough research to improve his or her life from multiple devices while not having to travel to meet with other community members (although, in my opinion, travel for meetings with other community members will soon emerge as a core reason for being a member of online communities).

Searching and Sharing

Communities are as old as recorded time itself. Religious organizations are one of the oldest types of community. They are based on members searching for spiritual truths and sharing them communally through prayer. Thus, prayer is user-generated data (the cost of goods sold of all communities, whether offline, online or mobile, is user-generated) and sharing it within a church membership has appealed to billions of people for a very long time.

Tribes were initially formed out of the need to search for and bring down very large game, which was then shared with members of the community for food, clothing and shelter. Churches and tribes have tithed for money or script as their principal source of operating capital and to keep their organization moving forward and growing. Tithing has served them well for thousands of years and it continues to serve them well.

City-states grew out of the need to channel water from rivers to farms and homes, and taxes were raised to pay for the canals, pumping systems, reservoirs, and storage containers and for the maintenance and defense of the water system. Governments were needed to raise the taxes and hire waterworks employees, and that's likely how civilization arrived at the need for centralized authority—the citizens were probably not sharing water rights fairly. Online communities have that problem as well, as you will see. Mobile communities have fewer problems associated with cooperation than do online communities, and there is a reason for that.

In modern times, millions of people have joined hundreds of thousands of communities that filled their needs. They pay membership fees and agree to serve on committees, thus contributing the three W's of community involvement: work, wisdom and wealth. Some of these community groups are well known to each of us to a greater or lesser degree—Rotary Clubs, the United States Golf Association, the Parent Teachers Association, the Sierra Club, alumni and fraternal organizations, the Cannes Film Festival, NASCAR and the National Softball Association, to name a few. Joiners are searching for something previously missing in their lives. Maybe it's to become healthier, or to improve of the beauty of the city, or to raise money for victims of a disease or to support the keeping of rifles in one's home. These communities do not post banners of automakers and beverage distributors in the meeting houses. Advertising isn't core to their purpose, and in fact would be a distraction. Their core purpose is to search, process and share.

In this book I take you through the various answers to the big question: Why do people join associations? We explore why this need burns in the breasts of many of us, and burns more vibrantly now that we are separated from co-workers and family because of telecommuting and spending more time on our computers and less and less time meeting with friends and family.

Persuading People to Join and Pay

If my message in *Smart Start-Ups* is to encourage you to form an online or mobile community, it is my responsibility, it seems to me, to show you how to make it economically sustainable and profitable. This process is known as building demonstrably economically justifiable business models, and I spend a fair amount of time in the book explaining the pillars of successful business models. That's fine, you say, but how do I get the customers to come to the community and to pay for the value proposition I present them with?

The first thing to do is to come up with the value proposition. Look at Mary Kay Cosmetics' value proposition: Let's get together at one of the ladies' homes to discuss our unattractive features and various creams and treatments to make them attractive. Or the Tupperware mission: Let's get together at one of the ladies' homes to discuss the various ways in which each of us has used Tupperware containers. Or the scrapbooking clubs' missions statement, which has resulted in hundreds of millions of dollars in sales of paper and leather materials, glues, tape and other accessories.

One of my favorite examples is the Billy Graham Crusade and similar evangelical tent meeting groups. If you haven't been to a tent meeting, I'm from East Tennessee and I'll tell you how the payment system works. At the end of the prayer meeting, where a lot of healing and shouting of "Hallelujah" has the crowd in a sweat, the preacher asks each member to light a candle and hold it in one hand, and with the other to pull out a five dollar bill and hold it over their head, then to close their eyes tightly while he leads them in a final prayer. A dozen of the preacher's associates walk among the believers and collect the money. The revenue model in the evangelical community is tried and true and proves that people enjoy the act of reciprocity—paying for the privilege of coming together and praying, shouting and singing to their Lord.

These community businesses find and hold on to members by using the precepts of Robert Cialdini's landmark book on persuading people to buy something, entitled *Influence: The Psychology of Persuasion*. These precepts are reciprocity, consistency, social validation, liking, authority and scarcity. If you employ a handful of them in the launch of your on-line or mobile community, and if the members see the value in what you are asking them to pay for, they will pay and they will persuade others to pay. Let me briefly explain these six factors:

1. *Reciprocity:* Everyone feels the obligation to reciprocate when they are given something for free.
2. *Consistency:* Once we have made a decision and that decision is validated by public affirmation, we rarely change our opinion.
3. *Social validation:* We often make decisions to purchase something if others validate our choice.
4. *Liking:* We often say yes to people we like, especially if they cooperate with us.
5. *Authority:* People obey authority figures because they think authorities know more than they do about certain things.
6. *Scarcity:* People frequently assign a higher value to scarce items, and companies that offer membership products on a limited-time basis know that scarcity commands a higher price.

I use the wisdom of other authors in *Smart Start-Ups*, when and where it relates to your ability to succeed in the launch and operations of your new online or mobile community. I also use my own on-site experience of seeking elegantly crafted business models brought to me by interesting entrepreneurs for purposes of seeking my angel capital group's investment. From this latter experience, I can tell you that there are some wonderful online and mobile communities in the marketplace and they are doing very well. Of course, the biggest and the best is eBay, and I dissect aspects of eBay's business model in the book. You may not have heard about the other rising stars: Cyworld, Habbo Hotel, Mixi, OhmyNews, SecondLife, Sonic Branding Solutions and Wikipedia. These companies, in my opinion, have the potential to become the next eBays.

No Cost of Goods Sold and Users Generate the Data

Some of the greatest businesses the world has ever seen and ones that have enormous staying power were formulated by entrepreneurs at their dining room tables when they didn't have a pot to pee in. If you take the bit in your teeth and launch an online or mobile community, it could be a very lonely process. I try to add to your enormous reservoir of courage by providing launch tools and rules to hang on to. I provide some guidance in the book, but you will be well served to study these four business models: FedEx, Electronic Data Systems (EDS), American Express and Weight Watchers International.

Let's look at their value propositions briefly, and I refer to them in the book because of their perfection. FedEx, created by Fred Smith from a term paper at Yale (he received a C for it), guarantees absolutely and positively that the recipient of your package will get it the next day. EDS, created by Ross Perot, is a facilities management company in which a group of people with certain skills call on a corporation that lacks those skills and is spending a lot of money to try to get something done. The group says to the corporation, "We'll deliver the solution to the problem you're seeking at the budget you're currently running, and if we do it for less than budget, we get to keep the difference." Perot's initial customer was Blue Cross of Texas, which couldn't operate its computers.

American Express charges up front for scrip in the form of travel insurance, which it calls Travelers Cheques, most of which are never used but, rather, stored away in members' sock drawers; and with this horde of cash, American Express launched a line of products for privileged members only. Most producers who place their products in American Express's catalogues pay for the pages. American Express collects the cash from purchasers, then places the orders with the vendors.

Weight Watchers International was formed by Jean Nidetch, because she was overweight herself and wanted to change her silhouette. Ms. Nidetch had a simple model: She would charge overweight women $2.00 each to drive to a downtown hotel conference room where they had the opportunity to stand up before other fat people and describe how and why they put on so much weight. As they left the conference room, Ms. Nidetch spread out a table before them against the back wall from which they could purchase cookbooks, recipes, cooking implements, calorie counters and so forth. Do you see similarities with the evangelists' tent meetings?

The thing these companies do so well is charge their users and members for providing them with a place to tell stories, share parts of their lives with others who are similar to them, remove concern about shipments of important documents, travel worry-free or try to become healthier. There is no cost of goods sold in these beautiful companies because the users prepare the data, the packages, the travel experience or the body fat. The combination is compelling: to create businesses like the ones I have just described, or ones modeled after evangelical tent meetings or Weight Watchers International, in which your customers pay you in advance and also incur the cost of goods sold. It is largely due to these two characteristics that online and mobile communities will become the greatest wealth makers in the history of entrepreneurship.

Tape this short message at the top of your computer screen: "My community will not incur cost of goods sold and my members will generate the data and pay me for the privilege of sharing it with other like-minded members." That will be the key to your success.

The Entrepreneurial Chase

I love the courage and creativity it takes to be an entrepreneur. I love the chase so much I have written 30 books on the subject. I am fascinated by the early stages of the entrepreneurial process, and thus invest at the angel capital stage. Ralph Waldo Emerson had an appreciation for the rookie as well, when he wrote:

> The most attractive class of people are those who are powerful obliquely, and not by the stroke; men of genius, but not yet accredited: one gets the cheer of their light, without paying too great a tax. Theirs is the beauty of the bird, or the morning light, and not of art. In the thought of genius there is always a surprise; and the moral sentiment is well called "the newness," for it is never other.

Mothers everywhere will encourage their children to become entrepreneurs once the age of online and mobile communities is in full flower, because the wealth creation will be startling. Nothing like it will have ever occurred in such magnitude, and dispersed to so many small towns in America, England, Europe, Israel, Russia, Korea, China, Japan and elsewhere. A community can be transported via language translation, and some adjusting for cultural customs, from one country to the next. OhmyNews, a successful Korean consumer journalism online community, is soon to be opening in America. Cyworld is coming from Korea as well; it is a cross between MySpace and YouTube, but on steroids.

If about now you're saying to yourself, "I want to launch one of these, but I don't know what to do next," take heart, for in Chapters 9 to 28 I describe a number of online and mobile communities that need to be launched, and I provide business models that I believe will assure their success—subject to your elegant execution, of course.

Disclaimer

As an angel investor in entrepreneurial companies, I attempt to sort the wheat from the chaff and select the best business models and the strongest and most interesting entrepreneurs who come to me for capital. Like the artisans in Plato's cave, I am chained in place all day, forced to stare at shadows cast on the back wall of the cave by various entrepreneurial teams. I choose the ones that I will invest in based on what their shadows remind me of, because I cannot turn around to see them or speak with them. It isn't an easy way to make a living, but it has its occasional rewards.

Several of the companies mentioned in *Smart Start-Ups* have found their way into my portfolio of investment shadows. (If you feel I am promoting them by mentioning them, I apologize, but examples were needed occasionally to emphasize a point. I don't name the ones I have invested in, because it could skew your thinking about the concepts that I present by citing them.) You are free to get in touch with me personally, and I will give you the names. E-mail me at *dsilver@sfcapital.com*.

Acknowledgments

WILLIAM SHAKESPEARE WROTE in *Measure for Measure*: "Our doubts are traitors, / And make us lose the good we oft might win, / By fearing to attempt." Laurie Harting, my editor at John Wiley & Sons, Inc., supported me from the beginning of the journey without fear or doubt, and to her I owe a huge debt. Fredrica Friedman, a dream of an agent, has been at my side throughout with powerhouse ideas and negotiating skills. Sophie McManus moved the project along with efficiency and charm and I am grateful for her assistance.

The staff at Cape Cod Compositors edited the manuscript with immense skill and patience. R. J. Quillinan burned the midnight oil grinding out the text and contributing the better word or the more useful phrase when needed. He's my champion.

Beginning with a blank canvas and Howard Rheingold's amazing book, *Smart Mobs*, it was my task to visit with entrepreneurs and gatekeepers in the world of mobile and online communities and ask them relevant questions. Many of the ideas and patterns in the book were woven from original thoughts provided to me by Rafat Ali, Scott Chumpelik, David Danon, Marty Gray and the staff at ProGames Network, Inc., Raph Koster, Clayton Loges and his Yodio team, Laritza Lopez, Sean Malatesta, Robin Richards, Lynne Saccaro, Caleb Silver, Claude Silver, Susie Progess Smith, John Szeder, Jay Wright—the "aggregator"—and Konny Zsigo.

If I were sufficiently brave, I would launch one of the mobile or on-line communities that I describe in this book. But I can't "do," so I teach best practices in launching them and select the best entrepreneurial teams to invest in. Thus, to all the courageous entrepreneurs with whom I have had the honor and privilege of working since I met my first champion of the genre, Senator Frank R. Lautenberg—who was building Automatic Data Processing with the Taub brothers above an A&P in Clifton, New Jersey—I thank you for teaching me the craft of entrepreneurship. You have given me a lifetime of joy.

D. S.
Santa Fe, New Mexico
March 2007

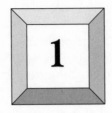

Introduction

If you've had a freakish education, use it. . . . An artist's only concern is to shout for some kind of perfection, and on his own terms, not anyone else's.

—J. D. Salinger

COME ONE, COME ALL to the greatest platform for entrepreneurial launches in the history of commerce! There have never been as many opportunities for first-time entrepreneurs of any age, 18 to 81, as there are today, and the need for capital to launch them is relatively small. With friends, family and a few angel investors, online and mobile community entrepreneurs can raise enough capital to pay for the launch and reach cash flow breakeven without selling valuable chunks of equity. Then, to pay for expansion, entrepreneurs can obtain most of their capital from members' float, from strategic alliances with content owners and from wireless carriers. Very little business experience is required in the coming three-year period, which some call Web 2.0, but which I call "the age of communities." If you have always wanted to start a company, you should do it now.

Very Little Capital Needed

There are essentially two kinds of communities that will be launched during this period: the online community and the mobile phone-based community. The first kind will aggregate members over the Internet, while the second will aggregate members over mobile phone networks.

The principal reason that you can launch an online or mobile community inexpensively is that the products or services shared in your community will be user-generated. This means that your company will not incur costs to make a product or deliver a service. Moreover, you will be able to bring users to your community without much of an advertising campaign. "Search and share" will be the overriding mission statement, and if what is being searched for is found, you can charge a subscription fee. Virtual marketing and search engine optimizing, plus word-of-mouth advertising about a massive new community, should be all that is needed to bring members to you. These marketing strategies don't cost much. Additionally, members' up-front payments will provide you with working capital, obviating the need for venture capital. In later chapters I show you dozens of revenue channels for your community, gleaned from successful off-line communities.

To reduce your need for assistance from friends and family or for angel capital, you may want to start a mobile community rather than an online community, because a mobile community has a major revenue channel not available to online communities: minutes of connect time collected by the wireless carriers that carry your content, of which approximately two-thirds will be paid to your company monthly. These sums can get huge, especially if your content appeals to teens whose parents pay their wireless carrier bills for them. Mobile communities are comprised of location-based users, the target of many consumer advertisers, and if your mobile users opt in to receive ads, you will gain a second revenue channel. Clearly the economics point to a world with more mobile than online communities.

Very Little Business Experience Needed

Don't be put off from making the leap into community entrepreneurship by the fact that you have very little business experience. Larry Page and Sergey Brin, the founders of Google, were studying for their PhDs when they decided to prove a hypothesis: that the totality of human knowledge could be put on servers and accessed by anyone. Google's revenue-generating model—ads placed next to relevant words—came later.

Pierre Omidyar, the founder of eBay, all of whose content is user-generated, had very little business experience prior to founding eBay. Omidyar's stated purpose was to see what would happen if everyone had equal access to venues of trade. Now eBay is such an enormously popular community that if it were a country, it would be the eighth largest economy in the world.

The first and most important tool is to borrow the fundamental mission statements of some of the greatest businesses ever created: eBay, FedEx, American Express, EDS, Weight Watchers International, Mary Kay Cosmetics, Lillian Vernon and Automatic Data Processing (ADP), to name some of the most sustainable. Their models can remain intact because of their demonstrable economic justification and the elegance with which their solutions are executed.

You will not be inventing a product, conceiving a new service, assembling a team of engineers or hiring an advertising agency to create community awareness. No, you won't be doing any of that. In forming an online or mobile community you will be aggregating users to share stories, artwork, designs, wisdom, songs, pictures, videos, news or other information, and they will pay you, directly or indirectly, for the opportunity to do it. Like the founders of religions, secret societies, unions, guilds, users groups, trade shows, seminars, fraternal organizations, associations, federations or groups, your task will be to convince people to come together to share part of themselves and to pay for that privilege. That will be your assignment, and I show you how to do it in this book.

The observation point that I have and from which I am able to support my hypothesis about the period 2007 to 2010 being the greatest period of entrepreneurship in economic history is that I am in my fifth decade of backing entrepreneurial companies. The notches in my rifle butt include such highly successful companies as ActMedia, ADP, Bobby McGee's Conglomeration, Codex, Frontier Telecommunications, FoxMeyer, IEC Electronics, Peachtree Software, Remington Brands, and Xing Technologies, among others—plus, the first tech transfer from a national lab. I have backed some losers also. You know those: the ones that you learn from as long as they don't kill you.

The Second Age of Communities

There are three legs to the stool of my premise that the age of communities will welcome millions of first-time entrepreneurs, perhaps such as yourself, like a giant vacuum cleaner, then slather you with angel capital and rocket some of you (the ones who pay attention) to great wealth. Moreover, there are a myriad of purposes, of demand curves, just sitting out there, waiting for entrepreneurs to form communities to fill the need, solve the purpose and create sustainable and valuable businesses in the process. The three legs of the stool are *collaborative participation*, *transfer of control* and *appearing to lack money*.

The age of online communities is the second age of communities in America. The first is the period from 1610, when the first Dutch immigrants reached what is now New York City, to 1831, the date of Alexis de Tocqueville's visit to the United States. In Russell Shorto's exceptional book *The Island in the Center of the World*, he describes the Dutch immigrants who colonized New Amsterdam between 1610 and 1650. Shorto cites a distinction between the necessities of the first wave and those of the second. The first group comprised infrastructure builders and commerce creators. They cut roads out of the forests, built docks, set up import-export offices, trapped beaver and sold their fur back to Dutch hat and coat makers, traded with the Indians and built homes and fortresses. The second group formed associations, guilds, schools, churches and communities, and we know many of their names—Brooklyn, Bronx, Secaucus, Hoboken, Peekskill, Fishkill and Poughkeepsie, to name a few.

To draw a parallel, the first colonists of the Internet were Internet service providers (road builders), Web hosters (retail infrastructure), retailers (Amazon, Expedia), security firms (McAfee, Norton), currency providers (PayPal), server and router producers (Cisco, Sun), message carriers (Sprint, EarthLink) and service firms (Google, Yahoo!, LendingTree, Match.com, Monster). The second wave of colonists of the Internet will be community builders. I will call you *communiteers* because you will see opportunities to create associations in which information, videos, games, music and research will be searched for, shared, massaged, organized, sliced, diced, discussed and catalogued.

The communities formed on the Internet and over wireless (and Wi-Fi) networks will grow into powerful purchasing-decision influencers, politician makers, politician breakers, and big institution topplers. They will grow to become the New Yorks, Philadelphias and Bostons of the pre-Revolutionary era. Their strengths will lie in their ability to attract millions of members, charge for services, stoke the inherent nature of people to cooperate, share files and prevent unwanted invasion pretty much like the minutemen of the Revolutionary War who held back the invasion of the Red Coats. Society and commerce will never be the same once the Internet and wireless networks are the land of the associations and the home of the communiteers. I predict the formation and sustained growth of 10,000 online communities, each with 1,000,000 or more paying members, and another 90,000 smaller online communities. *Each of us will belong to between 12 and 24 online and/or mobile communities by 2010, and our power to do good things and disrupt old industries will be unique and radiant.*

A Nation of Joiners

For as long as there has been record keeping of how and why societies of people cooperate with one another, we know that the reasons range from as simple as protection against enemies to means of capturing and killing larger game, to gathering enough people to play soccer, or to xenophobia. A reader of Umberto Eco's magical book *Foucault's Pendulum* can learn about secret societies from the earliest days to the present, cleverly woven together into an unforgettable novel.

The first observer of the notion that America was a nation of joiners was a French college student sent to America by his wealthy father to "do something useful." Alexis de Tocqueville, the Frenchman who studied American society in 1831, wrote:

> In no country in the world has the principle of association been more successfully used or applied to a greater multitude of objects than in America. Besides the permanent associations which are established by law under the names of townships, cities, and counties, a vast number of others are formed and maintained by the agency of private individuals.
>
> The citizen of the United States is taught from infancy to rely upon his own exertions in order to resist the evils and the difficulties of life; he looks upon the social authority with an eye of mistrust and anxiety, and he claims its assistance only when he is unable to do without it. This habit may be traced even in the schools, where the children in their games want to submit to rules which they have themselves established, and to punish misdemeanors which they have themselves defined. The same spirit pervades every act of social life. If a stoppage occurs in a thoroughfare and the circulation of vehicles is hindered, the neighbors immediately form themselves into a deliberative body; and this extemporaneous assembly gives rise to an executive power which remedies the inconvenience before anybody has thought of recurring to a pre-existing authority superior to that of the persons immediately concerned. If some public pleasure is concerned, an association is formed to give more splendor and regularity to the entertainment. Societies are formed to resist evils that are exclusively of a moral nature, as to diminish the vice of intemperance. In the United States associations are established to promote the public safety, commerce, industry, morality, and religion. There is no end which the human will despairs of attaining through the combined power of individuals united into a society.

Community Mobbing

You are going to be using the words *mobs* and *crowds* quite a bit in the next three years as new communities are launched and vast numbers of people sign on to the most useful of them. We will come to know this urgent and molecular need to join a group right now as something we are genetically prewired to do. This self-motivated wave of new joiners is known as *community mobbing* or just plain *mobbing*.

The phrase already has legs. Skype, the voice over Internet protocol (VoIP) telephony carrier, adds 220,000 new subscribers per day. MySpace.com, an online community of over of 110 million teenagers, receives 55 million visitors a month. Bebo, a San Francisco-based online community for teenagers, has passed MySpace in the United Kingdom. Facebook, an online community for the college crowd, has 15 million loyal members and has rejected an acquisition bid from Yahoo! of $800 million, according to the *Wall Street Journal*. Only in America. I would have taken the offer. Orkut, a community owned by Google, has surpassed MySpace and Bebo in Brazil, where it has a 70 percent market share with 39 million users. CyWorld, a South Korean social network, is approaching 30 million members. Piczo is big in the UK and Canada with 23.5 million members, according to *Forbes*.

The English language doesn't have a word that describes massive numbers of people joining an online or mobile club, so the club owners call it mobbing. Look for it in the next edition of *Webster's Dictionary of the English Language* as "the ineluctable and inevitable rush by millions of people to join online and mobile communities, therein to generate content and pay the communities' founders for the privilege of creating and sharing the users' content with others."

Mary Kay, Billy Graham and Jean Nidetch

I'll let you in on a little secret. Putting people into communities, having them pay for the infrastructure and selling space and having them advise one another on what to purchase and how the products pleased or displeased them is a 50-year-old phenomenon. It is known as multilevel marketing or party-plan selling and it was invented by the late Mary Kay Ash. Her company, Mary Kay Cosmetics, has unsalaried saleswomen who ask a sponsoring woman, the hostess, to invite her friends to her house for a Mary Kay party. The hostess pays for the advertising costs and provides the selling space. The invited guests pay the costs of getting to the hostess's home. The information that the attendees share is how to hide their unattractive features and enhance their attractive ones. The hostess receives a commission on all sales made at her home. Tupperware products are sold in this manner, as are sex toys and decorative wall accessories.

Another good example of user-generated content in which the members pay to swap information is the New York Stock Exchange (NYSE). It is the most liquid market for stocks and bonds in the world; in other words, the volume of trades is huge, thus the spread between bids and asks is narrow. NASDAQ is less liquid and is driven by computers, not by the bidding and shouting of members, and the spreads are greater. On the NYSE, the shout-out method has been the norm since 1645, when traders met under the buttonwood tree at the corner of Wall and Broad Streets in New York City. Corporations pay to have their shares and bonds traded on the NYSE and members pay for a seat. Men in their 80s still refer to the American Stock Exchange as the "curb" because traders would stand outside the exchange building on the curbs and shout out their orders to traders sitting in the windows. The traders would then *search* for the price that the market-maker *shared* with them, and a transaction would occur, or would not occur, depending on what information the trader and his customer on the curb shared.

In creating your community, remember that *liquidity* and *community mobbing* will be central to your success. If the members do not come in droves, shut it down, because it won't have necessary liquidity. eBay is a successful community because it has immense liquidity: Sixty million buyers and sellers essentially congregate on the front lawn of Pierre Omidyar's house to trade collectibles and other objects. It is perhaps the first online community, one whose business model and high ethical standards all communiteers should emulate. eBay charges sellers a listing fee and a sales commission. It encourages payment through its PayPal subsidiary. eBay has several other revenue channels, as well, some of which enable online communities, such as games, to operate with greater efficiency and liquidity. Look for eBay to segue to a mobile community format in order to block a competitor from capturing that market.

Online and mobile communities are an extension of another tried-and-true business model: *seminar selling.* In this model, people are invited to a conference room in a hotel where they pay to learn something that will make them richer, thinner, more spiritual, a better person or more likely to get into heaven. Billy Graham is the top seminar salesman in his line of work: evangelism. He can "pack a house," as they say in the entertainment business; 40,000 in Yankee Stadium was a low number for Dr. Graham in his heyday. I can remember him saying at the end of one of his electrifying sermons, "Now, y'all close your eyes and hold a five dollar bill over your head and someone will come by and pick it up, so we can keep this crusade for Jesus going. We want to take it to Germany, to Africa, to the Philippines and everywhere where people live in affliction." Reverend Graham's liquid North Carolina accent and the tomahawk chopping of his syllables were very compelling. The audience paid to attend. Dr. Graham provided the venue while the audience prayed and paid and thereby provided much of the content.

One of the best examples of a first-time entrepreneur who built an amazingly successful off-line community using a primitive, unsophisticated business model and message was Jean Nidetch, the founder of Weight Watchers International. Her business model can be summed up in one sentence, as she once put it: "I'm going to ask heavy women to drive downtown to a hotel conference room, then charge them $2.00 a head to stand up and tell everyone why they are fat, and at the end of the session, I will sell them products off a table at the back of the room." It still works that way, although the $2.00 is now $12.00. Weight Watchers was acquired by H.J. Heinz & Co. in 1982. It has a consumer recognition percentage of 91 percent, or considerably higher than any of Heinz's other products. If Heinz were a more entrepreneurial company, it would form an online cooperative community of Weight Watchers–type customers; instead, that opportunity will probably be grabbed by one of you.

User Groups and Trade Shows

All of us have been to industry trade shows. In the computer industry there have been users groups that in some cases morphed into trade shows. Hewlett-Packard and Apple Computer Company invented the users group in the late 1970s. They charged their customers a fee to join their users group—it was $500 per annum—for the *privilege* of providing them with ideas of how to improve their products. What nerve! Then once or twice a year, the users and economically involved people, such as makers of peripheral appliances and useful software, attended conferences at which vendors of microcomputer accessories rented booth space and knowledgeable speakers gave seminars in the adjoining conference rooms. Visitors, exhibitors and speakers all paid their travel and lodging expenses, and the users group sponsors made money in several non-core ways while gaining contact with their customers plus free research and development information.

In the 1980s, the users group conferences were copied and expanded by trade show entrepreneurs, such as Sheldon Adelson, who founded Comdex. Trade shows are one of the most profitable businesses ever conceived, because the entrepreneurs who own them merely pay for the rental of a large exhibit hall plus conference rooms in a city with a major airport, many hotels and entertaining night life. The ways that trade show entrepreneurs generate revenue are numerous, and include:

- Visitor admission tickets.
- Booth space rental.
- Sponsor fees—badge holder, shopping bag, coffee cup, pen, pad, cap, backpack and other souvenirs bearing the sponsors' logos.
- Advertisements in the trade show daily newspaper.
- Audio cassettes or CDs of the seminars and keynote speeches.
- Markup on hotel rooms purchased at a volume discount.
- Markup on airplane seats purchased at a volume discount.
- Sale of T-shirts and other paraphernalia.

What are the trade show sponsor's costs? They are relatively few and certainly small. They include venue rental; wages to people who check in the visitors, exhibitors and speakers; wages to guards; wages to janitor-ial staff; signage and advertising for the event; telecommunications, travel and lodging for the sponsor's staff. But with five sponsors each paying $150,000, hundreds of exhibitors paying $8,000 apiece and 20,000 visi-tors paying $400 a head, the hypothetical trade show's sponsor achieves gross revenues of around $2 million before the last five revenue sources in the preceding list are added in. After paying $50,000 to rent the venue and $150,000 in wages and other expenses, the profitability of a single show is around $1.8 million. *And all of the content is user-generated.* One of the oldest online communities, Wikipedia.org, which attracts lexicogra-phers and encyclopedists, has begun holding users group meetings once a year. These are natural extensions of online communities. And the com-munities that encourage physical meetings of their members are among the smartest of start-ups.

America's Favorite Pastime

Most online and mobile communities have a heavy fun component. They are happy places. Bear that in mind when you launch your online or mobile community. Ask yourself, "With which group of people throughout my life have I had the most fun, the most belly laughs, and the most joy?" We're all different, of course, but I will lay a wager that many readers will answer with some sports-related activity such as swim-ming, baseball or softball, cheerleading camp, golf, surfing, and so on. These activities are still going on, yet many would-be entrepreneurs overlook the fact that these events, enjoyed by young and old alike, are based on the participants generating the fun.

We paid (or rather our parents paid for us) to play Little League base-ball, attend hockey camp, join a softball league, attend swimming camp or join the volleyball or soccer team. Recently, entrepreneurs have started a professional baseball league in competition with the major leagues, to fill the demand for baseball in small communities. David Kaval and Amit Patel conceived the idea for a new baseball franchise while students at Stanford University, then engaged Kevin Outcalt, who invested the first $1 million in what is known as the Golden Baseball

League. There are more than 20 million people in America who play softball every summer in organized leagues, and an equal number of bowlers. All have fun sharing. Most of these amateur athletes would welcome a mobile community that informed everyone of events, notices, scores, player stats, ringtones, and places to talk about themselves, flirt and plan to meet. The United States Constitution is the only one ever to put the "happiness" of its citizens in its mission statement.

Membership Has Its Privileges

The greatest opportunities in online and mobile communities are smack dab in the middle of the older, wealthier members of society rather than with the 30-year-olds who continually and insatiably launch communities for the 18- to 34-year-old group. Teenagers and young people launching their careers have a pittance in their bank accounts compared with the 50- to 65-year-olds. Yet there are pitifully few online and mobile communities for the older demographic. That market is so large, it will welcome hundreds of communities in wealth management, estate planning, obituary writing, death management, nutrition, health, social entrepreneurship, search and more.

If you plan to launch a mobile or online community for this demographic, you can charge a subscription fee, and you can restrict membership to a smaller group of people who qualify. This demographic is quite used to exclusion, for financial or other reasons. Country clubs, eating clubs, gated communities and the American Express brand have been important icons in the lives of the 50- to 65-year-old demographic, and they are comfortable with paying where value is obtained. Also, this age group is not that needy of 150 new friends. These people want to manage their wealth, improve their travel experiences, share knowledge, improve search, live long and healthy lives, plan for retirement and, in the case of widows and widowers, meet people for romantic purposes. These needs warrant subscription fees.

Subscription fees can be higher if the community is set up for the privileged. It's a brand thing, and nobody has developed and protected its brand as well as American Express. It was originally a travel insurance company, selling something that many of us put into our sock drawers and forget about—travelers checks. If you look at American Express's balance sheet, you will see that the asset "Travelers Checks Outstanding" is $7.2 billion and net worth is $10.5 billion. To get paid in advance for a product that the customer may or may not use is called the brilliant use of float. In other words, most of American Express's capital is prepaid subscriptions to travel insurance that the customers do not use much.

Now, when you launch a community and charge a prepaid subscription, you are gaining float to pay for your launch, to hire people, to buy servers, to market your community to others and for overhead. When you add an upscale membership restriction caveat—only those who feel they can contribute to this community will be permitted to join—then you can increase the subscription from $5.00 a month to $25.00 a month, and this particular market will pay the premium for the "privileged" brand.

The first online community to restrict membership, Mixi, went public in September 2006 making its 30-year-old founder, Kenji Kashara, who held on to 64 percent of Mixi's common stock, a billionaire. Modeling a new community after American Express could be the smartest business move you will ever make.

The Rickety Scaffolding of the Early Online Communities

Pockets of wealth are being created before our very eyes. There have been a handful of online communities that have experienced mobbing already. The top 20 are listed in Table 1.1.

Note that these social networking communities are mostly teen-oriented. Most of them have received venture capital investments yet are still searching for sustainable revenue models. It is worrisome to me that many of the mobbed communities have not found demonstrable economically justifiable business models. They are permitting advertisers to place billboards on the roads shared by their members, but advertising is not core to the values of the communities. The founders of the earliest mobbed communities should take acquisition offers—as did MySpace—and laugh all the way to their banks. Aggregating large

TABLE 1.1   The 20 Most Mobbed Online Communities (Unique Visitors) through June 2006 (in Millions)

Name	June 2005	June 2006	Percentage Change
MySpace.com	17.7	52.3	195
Classmates.com	18	14	–22
Facebook.com	6.1	13.8	126
YouTube.com	—	13.4	—
Spaceslive.com	3.9	8.7	123
Xanga.com	8.1	6.8	–16
Flickr.com	1.1	5.9	436
360.Yahoo.com	—	4.7	—
LiveJournal.com	6.3	4.1	–35
MyYearbook.com	—	4	—
Hi5.com	3.4	2.1	–38
Tagged.com	0.7	1.8	157
Bebo.com	1.6	1.7	6
Friendster.com	1.1	1.4	27
TagWorld.com	—	1.3	—
Y3Things.com	—	1.2	—
LinkedIn.com	0.2	0.3	50
Orkut.com	0.05	0.3	500
XuQa.com	—	0.1	—
Cyworld.com	—	0.09	—

Source: Wall Street Journal Online, July 24, 2006.

numbers of people to share information about themselves does not, it seems to me, do anything more valuable than aggregate. The value of an online or mobile community has a lot to do with providing a search and share function, or search-process-share function, and one that is not easily duplicable. Nonduplicability equals disruptability.

The Strong Scaffolding of CyWorld

Cyworld, which was conceived in Korea in 1999, is attempting to reach the same market as MySpace by providing a more personalized approach to communication. The web site incorporates the MySpace features of community gatherings, search features for friends, and more. This community also borrows from online gaming sites, providing the ability to purchase artwork, wallpaper and other intricacies meant to make a user's homepage more personalized. The currency used is called *acorns*, which are purchased for $0.10 each via credit card or through Paypal. With these acorns, members use the "Shop" feature on the site to choose different enhancements for their home page.

The personal home page for each user is called their *minihome*. Inside each minihome, the user is allowed to personalize a *miniroom*. The miniroom has a .gif character to represent the user, and space to decorate the room to the user's liking. Possible purchases through the "Shop" feature include wallpaper, background, furniture, artwork, friends, animals and more.

The community provides several options for the users to join *clubs*, to reach out and meet one another. The clubs include those listed in Table 1.2.

TABLE 1.2   Clubs Available on Cyworld

Family and Home (39)	Romance and Relationships (61)	Fan Clubs (230)
Music (221)	Media (21)	Schools and Alumni (181)
Recreation and Sports (100)	Hobbies and Crafts (58)	Entertainment (142)
Religion and Beliefs (92)	Community (202)	Fashion and Style (112)
Education (49)	Career and Jobs (15)	Food and Drink (55)
Computer and Video Games (68)	Nightlife and Clubs (25)	Automotive (40)
Art and Literature (92)	Pets and Animals (52)	Government and Politics (16)
Business and Finance (33)	Sorority and Fraternities (13)	Organizations (41)
Science and History	Places and Travel (76)	Computers and Internet (62)
Health and Wellness and Fitness (27)		

Numbers in parentheses indicate number of clubs in category.

Summary

To assure yourself that you are selecting a marketplace that *needs* an online or mobile community, follow the lessons of legendary builders of communities: Billy Graham, Mary Kay Ash and Jean Nidetch.

Communities that have worked offline include:

- Religion
- Hunting and golf (a form of hunting)
- Beauty
- Weight loss

Communities should offer a scarce resource in order to set their members apart as privileged. Follow American Express's brilliant business model and restrict membership. This, and six other rules, will bring in paying members from the get-go:

1. Reciprocity
2. Consistency
3. Social validation
4. Liking
5. Authority
6. Scarcity

Finally, the community should be a fun place to join and search, process, and share with other members. Communities that lead to physical mixers where members get together are more sustainable because they solve the pain of loneliness better than do communities whose members always remain pseudonymous. Because their members want to be found by other members, mobile social networks are stronger business models than online social networks. They have more cash flow from strong payors, the wireless carriers, which reduces the amount of outside capital they need and will produce greater wealth for their founding entrepreneurs.

And above all else, your community must have liquidity: the sharing, trading or exchanging of fungible objects between members for real money, fun money, tip-jar money or synthetic money. Cyworld does this brilliantly. It could bypass MySpace inside of two years.

Collaborative Participation

We are transitioning to a new kind of culture. More open, more cooperative, more interactive where the focus of control passes.
—Kenichi Ohmae

The Need to Collaborate

Maybe it's in our genes, but human beings seem to need, in addition to food, clothing and shelter, a fourth factor to sustain us: collaboration. Before the Internet, we commuted to work along with all of our fellow workers, hung our coats up together, shared a coffee break, discussed our families and our weekends and gossiped about various topics of shared interests. The team concept was one of the leading business concepts of postwar commerce. Tom Peters described "management by walking around" among the teams as a key to success in creating a successful enterprise in his book *In Search of Excellence*, published in 1976. Today, thanks to telecommuting, people working from home and from Wi-Fi spots more frequently and in greater numbers, the need to collaborate is palpably urgent. We seem to have an innate social contract—an implicit agreement among members of a society to cooperate for a genetically required benefit.

Duke University professor Lynn Smith-Lovin surveyed 1,500 American adults on the subject of social isolation, and published her findings in the *American Sociological Review* in mid-2006. She found that people reported a sharp decline in their number of close friends, people they confide in, since 1985.

Twenty years ago people reported that they had on average four or five close friends. But in 2006, 50 percent of respondents told Smith-Lovin that they had two or fewer confidants, most often immediate family members. Nearly a quarter of the people surveyed said they had zero close friends. Research has linked social support and civic participation to a longer life, Smith-Lovin said. A social safety net of close friends is good for society. In an emergency, a person with few close friends has no one to turn to and ask, "May I stay with you for a couple of months?"

Collaborative participation on the Internet or via mobile phones is a way of reaching out to a social network to establish a group of close friends with shared values. Sure, it's not the same thing as playing golf with the same group every Saturday, or being part of a close team at work that parties together. However, people who bond in online and mobile communities are also getting together at live functions. Sonic Branding Solutions, a New York City–based provider of a mobile community that offers teenagers the tools to create their own ringtones, finds that many of the users gather together in the evenings and have ringtone dancing parties. "Our users create their own ringtones from turntables provided on our web site, TonemakerDJ.com, and then immediately want to share their creativity with their friends," says David Danon, Sonic's founder and CEO. Sonic charges its members $4.99 per month to create and share their ringtones, and it has signed up over 1 million members.

BuddyPing, a London-based provider of a mobile-based social network, whose goal it is to have people join and each bring in six friends, relies on the global positioning satellite (GPS) chip in mobile phones to link people together. For instance, one of my six friends is standing in front of a London movie theatre but doesn't want to see a movie alone. He SMSes (sends a note via short message service) to the BuddyPing network to see if anyone is nearby, says that he is a friend of David Silver's, and asks if someone would like to see the movie with him and then go to dinner. If someone responds, then a new acquaintance is made via the BuddyPing community. BuddyPing also charges members of certain communities in its membership monthly fees. People who want to know where their group is meeting this coming Saturday pay $9.50 a month to BuddyPing and also opt in to receive coupons and discount chits.

Communities are constructed by their users. Sure, an entrepreneur initiates the idea for people to come together to share stories, conversation, videos, music, information or research, but collaborators who join the community are the ones who build the community format and gather mobs of participants with buzz and word-of-mouth marketing. If the founder of the community target-bombs the users with ads, the users will be offended and will either demand that the ads come down or leave the community and go elsewhere.

The goal that a person seeks to fulfill in joining an online or mobile community is to collaborate with others who, like him or her, share a common interest. Through sharing that common interest, the joiner seeks to solve his or her problem: a vital need to collaborate.

What Makes Online and Mobile Communities Different

A number of factors make online and mobile communities different from their off-line counterparts.

First, in online communities the participants can use pseudonyms and thus can be bolder, for good or for bad. Mobile members want to be found. Second, in online communities the participants may not ever meet in real life, and as game theorists tell us, that means they are more likely to take greater risks and be bolder than if they knew they would meet others in the community some day (more on game theory later in this book). In mobile communities they frequently meet.

The third factor is that pseudonymity leads to noncooperators, called *defectors* who damage the community and must be discovered, exposed, tarred and feathered and sent out of the community *by the users*. Fourth, online collaborative participation models are disruptive to traditional industries. They will disrupt old-line companies and entire industries, with a trenchant force the likes of which we have never seen before. Off-line communities have occasionally disrupted existing institutions: Trade unions and the civil rights movement come to mind.

Online and mobile communities are *public goods*, in the economic and social sense of the term. They are places where people of like interests come to share stories, conversations, videos, music, information and research, and, through the process of sharing, make new friends. This is a perfect setup for wolves in sheep's clothing—for sex perverts to persuade teenage girls in teen-oriented communities to meet them somewhere, or for marketing departments of old corporations to plant users in the communities to recommend their products or services. These people are like vandals who graffiti public highways, or who throw rocks to knock out streetlights. They need to be rooted out, exposed, driven out of the community and publicly embarrassed by the users. I show you how that is done a little further on in the book.

The members of some online and mobile communities will tolerate a monthly subscription. These kinds of communities have large numbers of mature, intelligent and informed users—unlike the music and video communities, which are aimed at the 13- to 24-year-olds—who see the experience of collaborating as a duty, something of profound socioeconomic importance. SecondLife.com, an online community designed for adults to come together, ostensibly to trade mythical real estate but in truth to flirt and meet, charges an $8.00 sign-up fee.

www.ManyPeoplesChoice.com

The following is an example of a smart start-up that needs to be started: a mobile-based community that gathers consumer opinions from many people, affixes them to a radio frequency identification (RFID) tag stuck onto consumer products in supermarkets and drugstores, and lets the wisdom of crowds dictate product purchases. Users will SMS their first-hand experiences with cough syrups, allergy cures, pain killers, bug spray, and so on, into a central data bank, where purchasers will withdraw the information while standing in front of the products in Walgreens drugstores and other retailers. The company will be highly disruptive to consumer advertising.

Why will people join this community? To put a finer point on the question, why will people pay www.ManyPeoplesChoice.com $1.66 a month, or $20.00 per year (or any amount of money), to join this community? Because they believe that it will help to bring the best products to the forefront and push weaker products to the rear, and they believe that there are other people who share this need who will join ManyPeoplesChoice.com as well. Moreover, they will spread the word to friends and family members, as if it were a chain letter, that an opportunity exists to tell the truth and learn the truth from experienced consumers about a vast number of products and services; and that by reducing the requirement for massive amounts of advertising, the prices of these goods and services will fall.

And here's the really good part: People will be mobbing to pay $1.66 to join, plus pay for some cell phone minutes each month. Your share of cell phone minutes could be about $7.00 per member per month, if all members use the service once a day for three minutes. The founder of the community will split the revenues with carriers 60/40. Thus, if 1 million people join this community and pay $84.00 per year, and if Verizon, AT&T, Sprint, T-Mobile and others share 60 percent of the revenues from connect time with the entrepreneur, her company will receive annual revenues of $50 million and have very few expenses. Now, that's a smart start-up. I can see a lot of people signing up and a lot of consumer products vendors trying to plant decoy members in the community to publish producer-prepared copy. But the consumer products and services companies will not be able to penetrate the communities with self-serving reviews because they will be blocked by an armed guard created by the users, which I describe later.

What will be the upshot of the success of ManyPeoplesChoice.com? A substantial number of large packaged goods conglomerates will suffer sharp revenue declines and be forced to spin off, or kill off, the products that the ManyPeoplesChoice.com mob vetoes. The same model will work for insurance, mutual funds and annuity products, drugs, cars and trucks, sporting goods and travel packages. Giant media companies will lose advertising revenues and be forced to downsize. Many old media and communications companies currently appear baffled by and incapable of responding to the early smoke signals of the emergence of communities. The advertising industry will be radically downsized—driven out of town by the mob, as it were—and many of its large players will vanish. Interpublic, one of the larger ad agencies, announced radical downsizing on April 28, 2006, and as CEO Michael I. Roth explained, "We must be open to new, forward-thinking ideas that are responsive to the changing realities of marketing."

Control of the decision to purchase a good or service where personal taste is not a factor, but where benefits are, will transfer to entrepreneur-backed mobile communities. The future of consumer purchasing is in the mobile phone interfacing with RFID-tagged products, with consumers sharing information about the products.

First-Timers and Women Will Succeed

It is interesting to note that most of the new successful communities will be launched as start-ups by first-time entrepreneurs. This is the case because only entrepreneurs can be trusted to build public goods. Many old-line corporations have been deemed untrustworthy by people who have grown up with the Internet and mobile phones.

First-time entrepreneurs can be trusted to protect their users' interests. First-time entrepreneurs are deemed cooperators, not people who will sell out the interests of users, or rent their names. First-time entrepreneurs will ride defectors out of town on a rail and not carpet-bomb users with advertising. The major players on the Internet are not as trustworthy as are start-up entrepreneurs. As Bill Gates said in commenting on YouTube, an aggregator of 110 million viewers into a video community begun in May 2005, "We could never have done what YouTube did because of the copyright issues and the lack of a clear path to profitability. But I saw a bunch of old Harlem Globetrotter movies up there the other night, it's great."

Perhaps we should add a sister factor to the notion that a successful online or mobile community is built by collaborative participation: The conjoint factor is *trust*. And what businessperson is the most trustworthy? The entrepreneur. Why? The perception of naivete, nothing to lose, purity of objectives and rookieness. The age of communities will be captured by first-time entrepreneurs, because they are the only ones the marketplace will trust to build them.

Watch the Women Succeed

Men entrepreneurs usually think in terms of selling an interest in their companies for angel or venture capital. Women entrepreneurs, by contrast, frequently design business models in which float provides the operating capital; in other words, asking consumers to pay them in advance or up front for something they will deliver later.

Because they did not have the same access to capital as men, women have historically founded businesses in which the customer paid them in advance; i.e., trust-based businesses. I discovered this in writing *Enterprising Women: Lessons from 100 of our Greatest Entrepreneurs*, a few years ago.

Women will no doubt start more of the great online and mobile communities than they did first-stage Internet companies, because communities are trust-based and, as such, payments will be made up front to the community builders. These payments will sometimes, but not always, be monthly, quarterly or annual subscriptions. They certainly will not be advertising-based, because advertisers cannot be trusted and the glue that binds communities to their users is trust. Where there is trust, there will be float. Where there is float, advertising will not be necessary.

Float Your Start-Up on Float

The stage of conception of an entrepreneurial company is always exciting. A person identifies a large need, conceives an elegant solution to the need, and tells a sympathetic possible teammate with business experience the great idea for a new business. Soon the two entrepreneurs are begging and borrowing money, office space, computers and midnight oil to sculpt their new business. Unlike the waves of great, entrepreneurial periods of the past 50 years, the ones that relied on chips, modems or the discovery of DNA, the age of communities will rely on persuading people to share. Pick up a copy of Robert Cialdini's book, *Influence: The Psychology of Persuasion* for the recipe for persuasion. Further, to accomplish that, you will need to think like a 1910 union organizer working the sweatshops on Sixth Avenue in New York City, but using the Internet or the mobile phone rather than a bullhorn. Think Cesar Chavez, not Robert Noyce. Your need for venture capital will be very small, if any at all, since you will be asking subscribers to pay you subscription fees in advance of your providing a service and asking content owners to swap you their content for access to your mobs of users. This will provide you with float, one of the most beautiful words in the business lexicon. It means using the customers' prepaid subscriptions to finance the operations of your business.

Not all communities will be able to charge a monthly or annual fee. Fortunately there are dozens of other means of having your members pay for the use of your community, and I describe and explain all of them to you and cite live examples later in this book. But first, let's discuss six factors that you must first thoroughly understand in order to build a sustainable community for which members sign up in droves and in which they actively participate.

Credibility

Your community must be pure and honest. You must not shill for a corporate sponsor, because that will be discovered. You must vigorously keep untruths out of the information contributed by members in your community, as did Jimmy Wales, founder of Wikipedia, a not-for-profit community with 100,000 members who assist in incorporating all human knowledge on this Web portal. When an untruthful statement was made on Wikipedia by a prankster about John Siegenthaler, a distinguished journalist and former editor of the Nashville *Tennessean* newspaper, Wales instituted changes in the site's software and posting procedures.

A visitor to a community is "like a visitor to a public restroom," says Robert McHenry, a former editor-in-chief of *Encyclopedia Brittanica*, an off-line competitor of Wikipedia. "It may be obviously dirty, so that he knows to exercise great care, or it may seem fairly clean, so that he may be lulled into a false sense of security. What he certainly does not know is who has used the facilities before him."

If you want people to pay to come to your community and generate content with their time, and broadcast it to other members of the community, you must be known for maintaining a "clean restroom," to paraphrase Mr. McHenry. He was commenting on *Brittanica*'s arch competitor when he made the remarks, hence the somewhat pejorative analogy.

Ted Murphy, founder of a Tampa-based interactive agency by the name of Mind Comet, runs a side business, PayPerPost.com, that pays bloggers to say nice things about corporate sponsors. "An undisclosed PayPerPost placement on a little-seen blog isn't the most egregious thing out there," says John Fine, *BusinessWeek* media columnist. "But it's far from honest." Corporate shills, in my opinion, will be viewed as heretic by communiteers.

Classified advertising is user-generated content, and it has appeared in conventional newspapers for years. Readers write their own ads, pay for the inserts and purchase the newspapers to see their ad and the ads of others. Along comes another highly credible online community, Craigslist, founded by Craig Newmark, to take a big bite out of the revenues of newspapers. Newmark believes that "journalism needs to become a community service rather than a profit center," he told *The Economist*. Craigslist is for-profit, but it is highly credible because it sells no advertising and does not charge a membership fee.

Is it possible to both be highly credible *and* charge user fees? Yes, it is possible to do both. However, monthly or annual membership fees are not always an appropriate source of revenue in an online or mobile community. As the average age of the membership rises, subscription fees are more appropriate. There are dozens of other time-tested sources of revenue that are being used effectively by highly credible online and mobile communities. Stay tuned.

OhmyNews.com, a user-generated online newspaper in South Korea that has no editorial staff, uses the "tip jar" system that invites readers to reward good stories with a donation. Pleased readers click a little tip-jar button to have their mobile phone or credit card account debited. OhmyNews keeps 30 percent and the writer receives 70 percent. OhmyNews averages 700,000 visitors and 2 million page views a day. One particularly good article produced $30,000 in tip-jar revenues. Additional revenues come from advertising and syndicating the best articles to old media. It recently announced an English language version.

Google appears to be taking a page from Ohmy's book. In its proposed new service, Google Video, it will permit anyone to create a video which Google will then upload to all members of the community. It will let the creator of the video determine if he or she wants to charge for others to see it, and the creator can set the price per view. The creator will keep 70 percent and Google 30 percent of the fee.

Ewan MacLeod, one of the brightest young social network entrepreneurs in the United Kingdom who has built and sold a number of businesses based on parties, music and the mobile phone, recently launched www.SMSTextNews.com, a blog that reviews, discusses and rates mobile phones and their new features. Most of the mobile phone manufacturers send MacLeod their new models and he reviews them, and asks his blog readers to review them as well. A particularly helpful review is noted when a reader puts money into the tip jar as a way of saying to MacLeod, "Thank you for reviewing the latest phones from Motorola, Nokia and Ericsson. You helped me choose exactly what I needed."

Artists

Use a lot of art and as few words as possible in getting your message across. Artists lead cultural change and artists will become very important in conveying your message, which is essentially this: "There are benefits in cooperating; there is strength in mutual trust." Designers of your Web portal, or blog, or cellphone-embedded message will be critical to the successful launch of your new community. But wasn't that true of the Hudson Valley colonists who built attractive inns and taverns to host weary travelers? And wasn't that the case with haberdashers whose signage was simply a drawing of a hat affixed above their entrances? The 250-year-old Bird and Bottle, a bed-and-breakfast in Garrison, New York, still exists on Route 9, one hour north of New York City, and has a beautiful bright yellow façade with white colonial-style window frames and a white portico and soffits. Minimize the words and maximize the art. You may attract members more by the beauty of your message than the message itself.

In a study by the London Business School, it was found that "for every percent of sales invested in product design, a company's sales and profits rise by an average of 3 to 4 percent." In Daniel H. Pink's miracle of a book, *A Whole New Mind*, the Italian designer Gaetano Pesce says "customers will expect and want original objects in the future." Pink predicts that consumers will begin designing their own apparel and shoes. He cites a nascent effort at Nike (www.nikeid.nike.com) and at www.vans.com for Vans skate shoes.

There is so much media clutter today that you are much better off using *one word* to describe what your community stands for. We are being blogged, RSSed, pinged, e-mailed, IMed, SMSed, advertised to and offered music, online videos, mobile music and videos, movies, radio, print media and books. We are swamped with entertainment choices, connectivity to groups of like-hobbied or like-minded people, movies, opera, theater, dance, stand-up comedians and singers, circuses, preachers, self-help gurus, sporting events and our children's plays, dances and sporting events.

The only way for each of us to clear the clutter as possible community joiners, or to reach others to join the communities that we start, is by keeping our message down to *one word*. Okay, I'll cut you some slack—a three-word maximum, but one of the three must be a preposition.

Think about ads you have seen recently, and you will catch my drift. The Royal Bank of Scotland has chosen the Professional Golfers Association (PGA) Tour on which to run TV ads. Golf is a trust-based sport, in which there are strict rules of behavior. The PGA gives billions of dollars of prize money to charities. None of the athletes jump into the galleries to beat up someone who speaks during their backswing. It is a polite, honorable, steeped-in-history-and-heroes kind of community of viewers. And Royal Bank of Scotland has chosen this market to introduce its single, powerful descriptive word. And that word is "action."

Apple has captured the word "innovation." Volvo owns "safety." Lincoln Financial owns "Hello Future." Google owns "search." MySpace has captured "my place." The story of the launch of the jeans line Destroyed Denims bears some looking into. Christine Dolce, a.k.a. "Forbidden," a 23-year-old beautician, is now cashing in on her MySpace fan base of nearly 900,000 friends. Her online celebrity led to spokesmodel gigs for

Axe body spray and Zippo lighters. Then she inadvertently started a clothing line by posting a picture of herself in ripped-up jeans. They are more art than apparel. After fielding thousands of requests, Christine launched destroyeddenims.com, which sells mutilated jeans for $100 a pop. She is following this modest success by extending her line with posters, shirts and other gear. Christine Dolce kept it simple: Her name is "Forbidden"; her product is Destroyed Denims. There is a dearth of words, but a plethora of art and design in the miracle that Christine has pulled off. Check her out at MySpace.com and www.destroyeddenims.com. Her success is all about art.

Game Theory

You will want to become a student of game theory. Remember the movie *A Beautiful Mind*, the life of game theorist John Nash? Read his 1995 biography by Sylvia Nassar and that of John von Newmann. You will need to thoroughly understand why people cooperate when it is often in their best interests to compete.

When online communities are ubiquitous and tens of millions of people are sharing them continuously, peer-to-peer technology (P2P) will be called on to carry the messages. In a P2P system, the content is sent from client to client, without a server to cache and clean it. The sanctity of the content requires that the senders and the receivers uphold the standards of the community. It's like what we golfers do all the time, in every round.

It will be your steepest challenge to create benefits that reward cooperation and punish defection within the confines of your community. You may charge $20 a year as a membership fee and you may attract 1 million members; if so, your cash flow should be more than adequate to permit the development of devices to block noncooperators. The game theorists have some creative ideas for you, and I give you a handful of defector-blocking ideas as well, later on. You will have to learn game theory very thoroughly to block out corporate decoys, griefers, perverts and defectors. We will become game theorists together in the next chapter.

Primitivism

The need to cooperate is a primitive one. The cooperative community is as old as humankind, when hunter-gatherers went on hunting trips to capture and bring back precious foods and skins to the cooks, weavers and child-bearers so they could produce meals, clothing and shelter.

Because the need to cooperate is a gut instinct, you will achieve greater success as a communiteer by marketing to your potential members' guts rather than their brains. Simple headlines, crisp subheadlines, clear messages supported with impactful drawings and designs will gather more members than long, explanatory perorations. The hunter-gatherers drew pictures of their exploits on cave walls. Imitate that style because in doing so you are releasing control of how the community should look to the users who will want to make their imprint. A simple, direct message accompanied by basic artwork will absolutely appeal to the unconscious needs and wake up the desire, unaffected by objective reasoning, to join a group of people who share a common unspoken and thus far unstroked need. Remember this: Google's homepage began with just 30 words. Brilliant.

Winston Churchill used to imbed a phrase from the Bible into his wartime, courage-building speeches because, he said, "It makes the listener think back to when he first heard the passage. It was in Church sitting with his family. He was safe then."

Think of this little-known fact: The first of any work done by a creative genius is usually the most valuable. For example, Einstein's theory of relativity was his first and most important contribution to the physical sciences. Mickey Mantle's rookie baseball card is more valuable than any of his other cards or any cards in the modern era. Mantle was naïve, primitive, a rookie. The fans' love affair with him was enormous. Does Barry Bonds, an equally talented baseball player, have Mantle's prestige? No, because his skills are questionably chemically altered. Injecting chemicals into muscles to improve a baseball swing is not something that a naïve rookie would do. The earliest paintings of Roy Lichtenstein, Chuck Close and Frank Stella are worth more than their later works of art by a huge margin. Rookie-ness is an extraordinarily valuable property.

Maintaining a spirit of "just folks," not too bright, somewhat naïve, inexperienced and unsophisticated will attract members like bees to honey, and potential competitors will undervalue your effort, deride your company and leave you alone. You want that.

Geeks are socially primitive. Some of them make outstanding entrepreneurs. Bill Gates springs to mind. Dyslexic people make good entrepreneurs because they learn by integrating patterns. Charles Schwab is in that category. Schwab says, "I didn't know I was different until I was 12 years old." How naïve is that? Schwab has a huge fan club.

Pretend You're a Duck

This is a short tip. Ducks skim across the water effortlessly. They look so serene, so calm. But underneath the water line, where nobody can see, they are paddling like crazy. My message to you: Never let them see you sweat.

As a communiteer, you will be capturing the customers of some of the greatest consumer products and service companies in the world, and gathering them into crowds and mobs. Your communiteering efforts, if done well, will result in the mobbing of your community and the bidding of farewell by tens of millions of consumers to many giant consumer-oriented corporations. Your mobs will be ripe for revolution when you gather them into your army. Do not toot your horn about your achievements. Just skim across the pond like a duck and keep your mouth shut about what you're doing. The media should not be alerted to the success of your community until you have 1 million members. Read Sun Tzu's *The Art of War* or follow the tactics of Stonewall Jackson's Battle of Fredricksburg to learn the value of silence. If you need media praise, don't start a community. You will fail.

As a communiteer, your job is to conceive the need for a cooperative online or mobile community, a place where people will want to go at least once a day for two to five hours to share music, stories, conversations, data, documents, videos, research, ads, legal research, medical research, political ideas, event announcements and other information. *They will do all of the work.* The values and benefits in your community will be *user-generated.*

Yet you're going to make all of the money—carrier fees, membership fees, tip-jar proceeds, newsletter subscription fees, strategic alliance payments and up to 24 additional revenue channels, which I describe for you later. You will be leveraging the efforts of the crowd that you entice to come to your community and, in some instances, whom you persuade to pay $20.00 a year to join and share information with others. If you brag about your achievements, you will shoot yourself in your foot. Do not talk about your community to the media until your first $20 million of revenue or 1 million members has been achieved. Communiteering is for quiet entrepreneurs. If you need attention, take the next Greyhound to Hollywood.

Friendster, one of the first online social networks, and one that predates MySpace.com and Facebook.com, the two that are clear winners, at least for now, talked about its raising venture capital at a $50 million valuation in 2004; but that was before it had figured out a viable business model. *Business 2.0* reports that Friendster tried to sell itself to Viacom in mid-2006 for $5 million. It was turned down. Keep a lid on your story.

Reputation Management

Speech was created, we are told by linguists, in the form of gossip. Gossip was necessary to the members of the earliest communities so that they could discuss the sharing of the bounty, child-rearing techniques and tsk-tsk about violators of the standards of the community. And to this day, the function of gossip is to state and maintain the standards of the community. In the online communities that you will launch, gossip will be given a more highfalutin name. It will be called *reputation management*.

Wily consumer products and service companies will try to invade the forums section of your community and start a buzz about their products or services. They will be discovered through data mining and multiple regression analysis of data derived by collaborative filtering. Their attempts to corrupt the public good that you have built will be announced in the *newsletter* that you create. (More on the subject of public goods, and the means of managing the reputation of your community, later in Chapter 4.)

What Kind of Community Should You Create?

To focus your thinking on particular markets, ask yourself what kind of people you would like to hear applaud you three to four years from now when your stock begins trading on the NASDAQ. Or you might ask the question this way: What kind of content would I like to distribute through a new channel? Or alternatively, what industry do I want to bring to its knees and hear it beg me for mercy?

As I mentioned in Chapter 1, you can find terrific communities to launch online or via mobile phones by mimicking previously successful off-line communities. Your models are Weight Watchers International, Tupperware, Mary Kay Cosmetics, evangelical religions, seminar companies, self-actualization groups, associations such as the United States Golf Association, guilds, trade unions and scrapbooking clubs.

If you are virulently opposed to continued reliance on carbon fuels, here is a community for you to start. Let's say that you form a community called www.AlternativeEnergyIdeas.com and you state that its purpose is to gather together everyone on the planet who is fearful that our reliance on petroleum is going to destroy the planet. Let's say you attract 5 million members who pay $1.50 per month to share ideas on how to elect pro–alternative energy public officials, where to find ethanol pumps, how to convert automobile engines to run on corn oil, and so on.

Then one day, a member of your www.AlternativeEnergyIdeas.com community sends the following message to the other 4,999,999 members: "Fellow members: Let's boycott each of the major oil companies for 60-day periods. Here's my proposed schedule. Beginning next Monday, we boycott ExxonMobil for 60 days, then . . ." If all 5 million members participate, and each of them lives in a two-car family and each car consumes $50 of gasoline per week, the revenue loss to the oil companies would be $2 billion per month, or $4 billion for the 60-day period at the retail level. Big oil companies would certainly hear from their dealers. Do you think the big oil companies might be persuaded to change their business models if their bottom line was being attacked by an online power that they could not control? I think their CEOs would call in a consultant or two to discuss responses to the attack. If you start www.AlternativeEnergyIdeas.com, you should be the kind of person who was born without the fear gene, because you will anger a lot of wealthy and powerful people up and down the oil-drilling-to-gas-station pipeline. As the sign on an old, bumpy country road in Georgia reads, "Pick your rut well. You're gonna be in it for a while."

Do you love books? Or foreign languages? Or, perhaps continuing education courses? Maybe you would like to launch a new religion, or a new political party. People who buy old homes and renovate them could be nucleated into a community to share before, during and after pictures, to write stories about their adventures on old roofs, or in their basements with 150-year-old boilers, or about finding old coins under a floorboard. Or maybe you would like to make loans. Or maybe you like to help fraternal organizations with their newsletters and group travel. Perhaps your personal needs are met by helping children with their homework. Or perhaps you prefer big challenges such as delivering cutting-edge medical therapies to patients and their physicians who face tough, life-or-death options with older forms of treatment. User-generated content will be huge because there will be tens of millions of publishers, producers and distributors. Marshall McLuhan's prophecy is finally coming true: "Every man a publisher."

Strategic Alliances

Collaborative participation is not the only driver that will bring millions of people to your community, it is also one of the linchpins of your business model. When the urge to spend money to find more users comes over you, lie down for a few minutes with a wet washcloth placed on your perspiring forehead until the urge to do so goes away. You don't need to spend money to bring in more users; there are ways to bring them to you by collaborating with other communiteers and old content-owning corporations.

If I'm offering music on my mobile phone–based social network, then I will make a list of every organization with a theme song that might swap its song, which I may offer to my users as a ringtone, in exchange for my logo or web site beamed to their group.

For example, the New York Mets have a theme song that says, "Meet the Mets, meet the Mets, step right up and meet the Mets." And they have a huge screen in centerfield seen by all 45,000 fans at a sold-out ball game. Might the Mets advertise your online music community on their centerfield screen in exchange for your offering "Meet the Mets" as a ringtone song? I think they would, and so would other sports teams. As a Tennessee Volunteers fan, I would love my cell phone to play "Rocky Top" every time I got a phone call.

You might take this idea one step further and launch a community for sports fans to write their favorite sports memories. Sports fans are a special breed: They reconstruct their memories in a way that places them on teams, achieving greatness and adoration of fans. For revisionism on this scale, they will gladly pay a subscription fee. To find these fans by the millions, you could form strategic alliances with Division I and II college athletic departments to advertise your community on their video screens in exchange for their free license to read stories written about their teams, which they can publish in their game day books and on their web sites. Prizes could be awarded for the stories that receive the most votes. The prizes could be given by the teams—for example, 50-yard line seats to three games. *Unexpected rewards are absolutely key to creating successfully sustainable online communities.*

The opportunities for strategic alliances in the online and mobile communities markets are prodigious. There are multiple players: online communities with mobs of users searching for revenue channels; content producers of videos, music and games in search of mobs of users; consumer products and service companies in search of nonobtrusive means of reaching the new millennials (young adults who have grown up with the Internet), who have largely forsaken old media and its advertisers; wireless carriers who see dollar signs in their dreams from developers of mobile games; music videos that need a means of reaching customers; off-line communities whose managements are considering ways of morphing to the online and mobile world. If you control just one of these positions on this new Monopoly board, you can make deals to your benefit. Your need for capital will be minimized the more strategic alliances you enter into. A road map for negotiating strategic alliances is spread out on the table in Chapter 7.

Location-Based Advertising

Among the greatest opportunities to fall out of the sky and land, kerplop, on the Gucci loafers of advertisers is location-based advertising. But, they haven't *carpe diemed* it.

Most mobile phones are designed with global positioning satellite (GPS) chips in them, a post-9/11 change. And even without a GPS chip, a mobile phone user can be spotted via cell tower triangulation. This permits knowledge of the location of the mobile phone owner; for example, is she about to enter a restaurant? Is he standing in front of a shelf of printers at an Office Depot store? With that input, an advertiser can push a coupon, or a two-fer or an unexpected reward out to the mobile and capture a customer and the customer's number or pseudonym. The mobile owner need only opt in to receive ads. "Most of them opt in," says Dennis Crowley , the founder of Dodgeball, a mobile-based, location-based, opt-in-ad, social network serving active, out-and-about people in 22 cities throughout the United States. Consumer products companies will soon be lined up at the doors of the mobile-based social networks, testing various push ads, coupons and discounts.

The opportunity to be creative and collaborative, facing Coca-Cola, PepsiCo, Procter & Gamble, Hewlett-Packard, Unilever, JCPenney and Revlon, to name a handful of major consumer products and services marketers, has never been greater. If I owned a mobile social network with opt-in advertising, I would reach out to the planet's top 100 consumer advertisers and I would become their new advertising medium. If my mobile social network was composed mainly of teenage girls, the strategic partners that I would seek to do business with are those in Table 2.1. These are all of the advertisers that purchased full-page ads in the August 2006 issue of *Cosmo Girl!*

The mobile social networks and the advertisers listed here, and more, I predict, will soon be in a collaborative love fest that increases

TABLE 2.1   Candidates for Strategic Alliances Taken
from *CosmoGirl!*

Brand	Web Site
Mark Hookups	meetmark.com
PacSun	pacsun.com
Roxy	roxy.com
CoverGirl	covergirl.com
American Eagle Outfitters	ae.com
Clinique	clinique.com
K. Swiss	kswiss.com
Maybelline	maybelline.com
Redken	redken.com
Buckle	buckle.com
Neutrogena	neutrogena.com
Converse	converse.com
L'Oreal	loreal.com
Revlon	revlon.com
Ralph Lauren	polo.com
Stay Free! magazine	stayfreemagazine.org
Vans	vans.com
Old Navy	oldnavy.com
Zinc	zincclothing.com
Aeropostale	aeropostale.com
Livs	livs.biz
JC Penney	jcp.com
New York Film Academy	nyfa.com
Unionbay	unionbay.com
St. Ives	stives.com
Abreva	abreva.com
Secret	secret.com
Clubzed	clubzed.com
YMI	ymijeans.com
Playtex	playtextampons.com
Tyte	tyte.com
Wal-Mart	walmart.com
Bobby Jack Brand	bobbyjackbrand.com
Nature's Cure	naturescure.com
Flex	flexonline.com
Ben & Jerry's	benjerry.com
Tampax Pearl	beinggirl.com
Clean & Clear	cleanandclear.com

brand trust by association, sales and customer loyalty for the brands while boosting revenues, float and capital for the mobile social networks.

Some marketing ideas for these corporations using the mobile social network channels are provided in Chapter 8 and in the prescriptive chapters, 9 through 26.

Consult Rather than Communiteer

If you are not cut out to be an entrepreneur, or if you are not interested in starting up a unique new enterprise, you can thrive as a repairman for industrial giants that will not see the wave coming, or will see it but ignore it. Giant corporations are very slow moving, and rarely rewrite their business models, even in the face of obvious direct threats to their very existence, which communiteering will most certainly become. Their CEOs haven't heard about the emergence of the formulation of consumer groups that could boycott certain products or services. Many of them haven't heard of mobile social networks, although they pay their daughter's mobile phone bill every month. But listen to this community power idea for a few seconds and see if you agree with me that it is feasible.

Virtually every consumer-oriented company, from Procter & Gamble to Time Warner, will need to revise its business model and its mission statement, because of the tectonic shift in how goods and services will be bought and sold five years from now. Instead of being a major consumer products or service company, many of today's industry giants will be toppled by the power of communiteers. Consultants who catch the wave will make fortunes rewriting business models for the Fortune 500. But the inertia of many of their well-paid managers will delay the speed at which they change to catch the wave, and the wave will drown them. Your task, Mr. or Ms. Goodwrench, is to get there before they collapse and rewrite their business plans for them.

It is abundantly clear from scrolling through the top 10,000 most-visited web sites on Alexa.com, an authentic scorekeeper of which sites receive the most unique visits, that large, established corporations do not receive many hits. Nothing in my research persuades me that they will ever attract and sustain many visitors. The reason is that they are not new; they aren't rookies; they aren't primitive; they aren't fresh, novel, fun, high-spirited; and they aren't perceived by millennials as trustworthy. Established corporations—and this includes those that are 2 years old or 200 years old—are not trusted by the kinds of people who use the Internet as their primary source of entertainment, information, research and knowledge.

If you consult for older corporations you will want to dress up their web site, of course, but your charge will be to introduce *experiential marketing* to the suits. This means creating a Da Vinci Code type of search for the corporation's new product—a car, a truck, a line of apparel, a soft drink—giving numerous clues to the location as to where the new product is hidden, and a prize for those who find it. You will want the people who join in the search to team up with others and write stories about the fun and funny things that happened to them while they were on their journey. The winning stories will be published on the corporation's web site, and the authors of the three best stories will receive prizes of $5,000, $3,000 and $2,000 respectively.

The experiential marketing game can be done twice a year, once in summer with the prize hidden in or near a fabulous beach resort, and once in winter with the prize hidden in or near a well-known ski resort. A community can be formed of the searchers; friends can be made along the way, and the members of the community can be nucleated into a users group to comment on, critique and improve the corporation's product.

Audi did this in conjunction with Intent MediaWorks, Inc. (www .IntentMediaWorks.com) to introduce its new A2 automobile. Audi gave 29 increasingly more difficult clues and the winner received a new A2. Microsoft launched its Xbox 360 in 2006 with an experiential marketing search that ended in the Mojave Desert, where their partner Best Buy built a faux retail store for the launch. Both corporations were pleased with the results.

The message to old corporations is that new tools have been created to enable consumer products and services to be marketed to consumers who hold these tools in their hands—mobile phones and laptop computers. The ubiquitous BlackBerry is so vital to the young business person that it is sometimes referred to as the *crackberry*. The two sides, marketers and communiteers, will soon reach out to each other and form unique and profitable alliances if—and this is a big if—they adopt innovative marketing methods. If they use a lot of art, trust-building schemes, primitive design and game theory logic, the old corporations may yet become credible to the millennials in the approaching era.

Consumer Finance

We are starting to see community mobbing in consumer service markets. You know the ones: They have phrases like "points," "closing fees," "renewal fees" and "collateral management fees." These markets are perfect for a takeover by community mobs. In consumer loans, a traditional industry, two start-ups, Zopa.com in the United Kingdom and Prosper Marketplace (Prosper.com) in the United States, are bringing individual borrowers and lenders together.

Borrowing techniques from microlending, where small loans are made to seamstresses and grocers by the World Bank and others, on the web portals of Zopa.com or Prosper.com lenders form groups to bid on loan requests by borrowers, whose creditworthiness is certified by the clearinghouses. The rates are less than those charged by credit card companies and commercial banks. Because the transactions occur on the Internet, the borrowers receive immediate money. Zopa and Prosper Marketplace say that lenders can earn a higher rate than they would from a savings account and borrowers pay less than on a credit card. According to Richard Duvall, Zopa's chief executive, interest rates on Zopa have averaged 7 percent before bad debts (of which there have so far been none). That compares with the 4.5 percent paid on a savings account and the 15 percent typically charged on credit card debts.

There is a psychic payoff, too. Users on Zopa have said that they like lending and borrowing within a community of "real" people, rather than through a faceless bank. Mr. Duvall noted that affinity credit cards (i.e., those linked to an activity or membership) tend to have lower default rates than traditional credit cards. "The sense of community matters," he said.

Now picture these two start-ups being emulated by tens of thousands of other Internet lender clearinghouses that form lender groups, and you can see, perhaps, the wave coming ashore that will create an entirely new industry of online, instantaneous loans and e-wallets.

E-Wallets

I just threw a buzzword at you, *e-wallets*, so let's stop to define it and state its purpose. In the online world we cannot pay with cash, and we can't mail a check. Thus, the form of payment most accepted by online merchants and most preferred by online consumers is the credit card. For online gambling, an area that Discover and American Express will not touch with a 10-foot pole, and which Visa and MasterCard are not thrilled about, a handful of entrepreneurial companies have sprung up to process the bets of online gamblers. These companies are called e-wallet companies. The best known of them is six-year-old NetTeller. Its stock trades on London's AIM (like the United States' NASDAQ) at a market cap of £650 million on revenues of £170 million.

It's worth becoming an e-wallet company, and I can tell you how to do it and why it's worthwhile. The reason it's worthwhile is that there are multiple cash flow channels in the credit card processing business. For example, there may be a charge of $2.50 when money is deposited into the card; $1.50 to $2.50 when the card is used at an ATM; $3.50 (on average) when the card is used to make a $100 purchase; $0.05 when the card is used to make a phone call; $5.00 when the card is used to effect a money transfer; $25.00 over-limit fee; $25.00 annual fee; and so on.

If you intend to launch a community, your members will be proud of their shared wisdom in joining the community, particularly in the early days. They will be evangelists for the guild, group, storytelling club or quilting bee that you have started, and they will gladly accept and proudly use the community's credit card. Remember to say in the headline offering the card something along the lines of the Ben & Jerry's Ice Cream promise, such as "10 percent of every purchase made with your MortgageLenderCommunity.com credit card will be sent to Doctors without Borders, Save the Children Federation or World Health Organization," or the pledge of your choice.

The "how" one gets into the affinity credit card business is not that difficult. You can certainly contact NetTeller (the stock symbol on Yahoo! Finance is NET-L), Trade Group or WebTrades, the three largest e-wallet companies, exclusive of PayPal. Obopay.com recently raised $10 million in venture capital to develop an e-wallet system.

A very flexible card is the one offered by GenieBancor.com. It is known as a merchant card (identical to PayPal in that respect) and as a prepaid credit card, a money transfer card and a phone card. Any communiteer who licenses this merchant card and offers it to his or her members will be pleased with the adjunctive cash flow the card will throw off. I use the card in my business and, to paraphrase my late friend Victor Kiam, who bought Remington Brands in a leveraged buyout because he liked its electric shaver, "I liked the card so much, I invested in the company."

Think about Zopa and ProsperMarketplace for a moment. There is no currency involved. It's e-money moving from one e-wallet to another e-wallet. Toss the notion of "no more hard currency" around in your brain for a few minutes. What currencies are growing in importance? First, there are frequent flyer points. Collectibles such as baseball cards represent three-days-to-currency on eBay. There are also frequent shopper points; "slot points" earned at off-line casinos; symbolic wealth, such as Palladium Gold, created on the massively multiplayer online role-playing game EverQuest II; Linden dollars earned at SecondLife.com; and Kudos earned on CokeMusic and Habbo Hotel. The buildup in alternative forms of cash—which is inevitable because buyer and seller meet pseudonymously and not in person—begs for a single swap meet where the new currencies can be traded, bought and sold and swapped.

A Foreign Exchange Market

If you go with my suggestion of creating a private-branded e-wallet to be issued to the users in your community—and I heartily recommend it because of its many noninvasive revenue channels—the next step is to enable your users to bring currencies other than their national currencies to your community to trade with. For instance, permit them to use curren-cies earned in mythical worlds such as Linden dollars and Palladium Gold. Let them use sports trading cards, slot points, frequent flyer points, frequent shopper points and foreign currencies. If I am The Gap, I would let players bring their Palladium Gold to buy jeans at my store, knowing I can convert the mythical money to real money on IGE.

Edward Castronova, an economist who studies mythical worlds, places the amount of mythical money exchanged each year at $800 million, and growing. eBay was grossing $30 million in revenue per year by exchanging Palladium Gold, a mythical currency, for U.S. currency until it shut down this window on January 31, 2007, allegedly because of too many fraudulent trades. This leaves IGE as the only operator of a market for the exchange of synthetic assets and currency. Setting up an auction market in multiple currencies is not difficult for computers and their programmers.

It isn't out of the question for your community to offer cash prizes, fees for spotting and outing wolves in sheep's clothing that pretend to join your community but in fact are pushing their corporation's product or service. You might consider using a private-branded currency because people tend to spend it more freely. Don't we spend more of a foreign currency when we are on vacation? Yes, because we are more relaxed and in a buying mood.

We Want BetterSearchResults.com

Have you ever seen a company make as many acquisitions and do as much rapid diversifying as Google is doing? I haven't. Google is rumored to have offered Facebook.com, the college student community, more than $1 billion to acquire it. It is clear to me that Google is running away from its core business—the immediate placement of relevant ads next to key search words—as fast as its young legs can carry it. I believe it is attempting to diversify because the advertising business has peaked for Google and its growth has hit a ceiling.

A second reason perhaps is that Google's search accuracy is not very good. It brings back the correct answer or response to a typical query 34 percent of the time, according to a study by Linda Sherman of IDG. A search engine developed by Quigo, an Israeli firm, which licenses Yahoo! and others, brings back the correct response to a query 94 percent of the time. It is 2 percent better than the search engine developed by Cognition Technologies, Inc., in Santa Monica, California, used by litigation attorneys who need to power through hundreds of thousands of documents per hour prior to taking depositions or going to trial. A community is just sitting there waiting to be formed for members who want the *correct* answer to a query, and not 1 million *possible* answers to a query.

Collaborative Crowds

I think the time has come to bring together people who do a lot of searching, for the purpose of helping one another find the right answer to a query 100 percent of the time. There are 16 popular Web-based search companies, but most of them are not very accurate. Crowds are more accurate than experts when it comes to searching. As I learned in reading *The Wisdom of Crowds* by John Surowiecki, a community will always do better than an expert when it comes to a search.

If it is your serious intent to launch an online or mobile community, be sure to check out the bibliography that appears at the end of this book. I rented the minds of a gaggle of brilliant thinkers and provided them for you to integrate into the business plan of your new community. Let me spend a minute or two on *The Wisdom of Crowds* because its message goes to the heart of why user-generated searches, story ideas, advertisements, designs and information are nearly always better than those generated by experts. Surowiecki uses many examples to prove his point, and although he doesn't say directly why crowds are finally getting their say with blogs, podcasts and community-generated story ideas, it is time that in the age of communities the crowds are finally being listened to. And their story ideas are being listened to by old media. Paramount, the moviemaking division of Viacom, Inc., prereleased the Samuel L. Jackson movie *Snakes on a Plane* to several online communities, and the crowd made 30 changes, all of them adopted by Paramount. The crowd also wrote the movie's theme song. The changes were so significant that numerous scenes were shot a second time, and the movie was changed from a PG to an R rating.

Surowiecki also writes about crowds of miner families who picked the correct spot where several miners were trapped underground, while experts failed at the task. So much for experts in the age of online communities. It goes without saying that I picked hundreds of brains from out there in the crowd before writing this book.

What is it about the crowds that make them think collaboratively, toward a common goal that benefits everyone, not merely each individual? Are we genetically wired at birth to prefer collaboration over competition? We don't need to know the answer to succeed as communiteers, but when we get to the game theory section of the book, the opposite view is proposed: that we are genetically wired to compete, but that in certain instances, cooperating trumps competing.

Surowiecki tells the following story in *The Wisdom of Crowds* about the wisdom of a crowd of law students. (Is there a group of people more programmed to compete tooth and nail than law students? Probably not.)

In 1958, the social scientist Thomas C. Schelling ran an experiment with a group of law students from New Haven, Connecticut. He asked the students to imagine this scenario: You have to meet someone in New York City. You don't know where you're supposed to meet, and there's no way to talk to the other person ahead of time. Where do you go?

This seems like an impossible question to answer well. New York is a very big city, with lots of places to meet. And yet a majority of the students chose the very same meeting place: the information booth at Grand Central Station. Then Schelling complicated the problem a bit. You know the date you're supposed to meet the other person, he said. But you don't know what time you're supposed to meet. When will you show up at the information booth? Here the results were even more striking. Just about all the students said they would show up at the stroke of noon. In other words, if you dropped two law students at either end of the biggest city in the world and told them to find each other, there was a very good chance that they'd end up having lunch together.

Schelling replicated this outcome in a series of experiments in which an individual's success depended on how well he coordinated his response with those of others. For instance, Schelling paired people up and asked them to name either "heads" or "tails," with the goal being to match what their partners said. Thirty-six of forty-two people named "heads." He set up a box of sixteen squares, and asked people to check one box (you got paid if everyone in the group checked the same box). Sixty percent checked the top left box. Even when the choices were seemingly infinite, people did a pretty good job of coordinating themselves. For instance, when asked the question: "Name a positive number," 40 percent of the students chose "one."

How were the students able to do this? Schelling suggested that in many situations, there were salient landmarks or "focal points" upon which people's expectations would converge. (Today these are known as "Schelling points"). Schelling points are important for a couple of reasons. First, they show that people can find their way to collectively beneficial results not only without centralized direction but also without even talking to each other. As Schelling wrote, "People can often connect their intentions and expectations with others if each knows that the other is trying to do the same."

What am I proposing? I am pushing one of you future communiteers to launch a user-generated search community where the wisdom of crowds will bring back the accurate answer to a query 99 percent of the time. Forget the 1,110,000 responses to the query "venture capital" that Google provides. Forget the relevant ads placed next to the responses that Google, Yahoo! and others sell to generate their revenues. That's so yesterday. In a user-generated search business model, the users pay a subscription fee of $20.00 per year to have the mob answer their queries and for the privilege of answering the queries of the other members.

Online boat and boat accessories retailer iboats.com has a 1,200,000-page Web portal and is clearly the leading online boating community as well. iboats currently lists over 350,000 different boating-related products totalling 1,800,000 SKUs (a Wal-Mart supercenter has about 110,000 SKUs), and it is this huge inventory that has attracted such a huge number of monthly visitors to the iboats site: upwards of 4,000,000 people a month. A community has evolved, and every year 200,000 unique visitors to the iboats forum page post new questions. They range from "How do you get your wrench to hold on to a Johnson 60 hp engine when your boat is bucking in high water?" to "Where's the best cove to look for smallmouth bass on the Tennessee River near Alcoa?" In one year, 1,000,000 responses are provided to the 200,000 questions. These numbers are growing at the rate of 5 percent per month, according to Bruno Vassel III, the company's CEO.

Frequently, we need an answer to a question when we are on the fly. We are running to a meeting and the woman we are pitching, we have learned, is a serious collector of Esther Williams memorabilia. We need to know the name of Esther's husband, the cross-dressing actor, in order to demonstrate an interest in the field of interest of the important woman executive we are about to meet. We text the question to the mob, and if they are as helpful as the iboats crowd, the answer will come back before we ring the executive's bell. I would make this community mobile phone–based, because it will bring in money from the carriers for the numerous minutes of connect time.

Making and Distributing Movies

Azureus.com, an online community for viewing movies, playing games and listening to music, could be the harbinger of the future business model of the movie business. The current model, which is based on using releases in movie theatres to stimulate DVD sales, is tattered and broken. The largest movie-viewing demographic wants to see movies on their PCs, digital video recorders (DVRs) or cell phones. Like an elephant trying to turn around in a bathtub, moviemakers are slowly responding. Independent movie producers are going to bring the major motion picture distributors to their knees using P2P platforms, incorporated with a reputation manager that goes by the acronym *DRM*, for digital rights management.

A movie production and distribution company called 2929 Entertainment, founded by Internet entrepreneurs Todd Wagner and Mark

Cuban, released *Bubble* simultaneously in movie theatres and by P2P in January 2006, with the DVD version following four days later. Mark the day, ye movie goers; for it is the day the distribution method changed forever. This form of distribution, known as *universal release* breaks the mold in which films are released in discrete windows—first theaters and then months later on DVD and then cable and free television. Because movies are shot digitally, they can be released to personal computers with a click of a key, thus saving millions of dollars in distribution costs. *Bubble*, a Steven Soderbergh–directed film, is the first of a dozen films that Wagner and Cuban have in development.

Permit me to digress. Here's a little quiz to see if you've been paying attention. Why will distribution move to online communities from movie theatres and DVDs? Because they are an art form. Art leads cultural change. People who like the same kind of movies probably enjoy sharing movies with one another. Movies are a primitive form of relaxation; we forget our problems for two hours to view the problems of others.

In the P2P world, everyone can be a digital movie producer/distributor and everyone can download it, pay for it and view it. How primitive is that? People like to tell their friends when they've just seen a great movie—that's sharing. Downloading digital movies to communities of first-release viewers—a Sundance Film Festival moved to an online community—is an idea waiting to happen. Someone jump into this opportunity, and sign me up for film noir, please.

Unlike Wagner and Cuban, who sold Broadcast.com to Yahoo! for $5.7 billion, you will need to raise capital to form an online community to distribute first-release and indie movies. You will also need one or two brilliant software persons who have skills that complement your enthusiasm and skills. If you come from the shoe business and want to disrupt that industry by forming a community of shoe fetishists, then the businessperson you hire should have finance and business development skills honed in the shoe business. Four people, four computers, one big idea, a broadband link to the Internet, a lot of courage, integrity, creativity and about $350,000 in angel capital to carry you to product release is what you need to begin. How do you raise $350,000 in angel capital? How much ownership need you give away for the capital? You may not have to raise very much. Strategic alliances bring in float and capital. Collaboration, to put a sharper point on it, brings up-front money that obviates your need for angel or venture capital. You will find answers in Chapter 7.

But will you succeed? In Chapter 6, I describe the 11 criteria necessary to create a successful business model. Each of the criteria is assigned a value; the higher the cumulative point score that your business model earns, the greater the likelihood of your success.

After you plow through the eight platform, groundwork and process chapters, the remainder of the book—19 chapters—is devoted to wonderful new entrepreneurial opportunities for you to consider launching. Follow me, you colonists of the age of communities.

Summary

- In forming your online or mobile community, rely on the *wisdom of crowds* to generate the community's data. User-generated data equates to no cost of goods sold, which means larger profits.
- Rely on *strategic alliances*. If your community owns content, ally with aggregators of relevant mobs; if your community contains mobs, tether yourself to social networks that own content.
- Your primary capital is *trust*.
- Members will provide you with *float* if you remain credible. Women entrepreneurs have done this for centuries.
- Use a lot of *art* and few words.
- Think *primitivism*; do not be sophisticated.
- Manage your *reputation* aggressively.

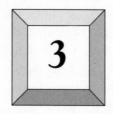

Transfer of Control

"Hold your tongue!" said the Queen, turning purple.

"I won't!" said Alice.

"Off with her head!" the Queen shouted at the top of her voice. Nobody moved.

"Who cares for you?" said Alice (she had grown to her full size by this time). "You're nothing but a pack of cards!"

—Lewis Carroll, *Alice's Adventures in Wonderland*

Who Stole My Customers?

To use the Lewis Carroll story as an analogy, the Queen today represents old media and old consumer products and services companies. Alice represents entrepreneurs who launch online and mobile communities.

On the community site Threadless.com, shoppers rate and buy T-shirts designed by other users and suggest ideas for new designs. Etsy.com, a community for handicraft creators, lets its users vote on which products should be featured on its homepage. And Slim Devices, an electronics maker, lets members sell their open-source software plus accessories for its digital music gear. Etsy works like eBay and takes a 2.4 percent slice on product sales, but its users determine how products are displayed. In less than a year, Etsy has attracted 10,000 sellers and 40,000 buyers.

Threadless.com runs a daily T-shirt design contest and pays $750 to the winning designer plus $250 in gift certificates. It then prints 600 of the winning T-shirts and offers them on its site for $15 apiece to the members who voted for it. If it sells all 600, Threadless earns $9,000 less the $1,000 it paid out to the winning designer. Co-founder Jake Nickell told CNN that the company took in $6.5 million in 2005. "Our users have the ability to change the company whenever they want," Nickell says, "because they make all decisions, from what we sell, and how much we sell. We just shepherd the decisions to the community."

Old Media Just Doesn't Get It

When two or more people are having a conversation, the speaker is usually selling and the listener is usually buying. For nearly 80 years in the case of radio and 50 years in the case of television, we have "bought" whatever a very small group of creative people and their suits determined we should listen to and watch. If they could get sponsors to pay for it, they sold it to us. A handful of people at ABC, CBS, NBC, the BBC and more recently the cable TV companies have dictated the subjects of our conversations for 80 years.

Now, the tables have turned. The *millennials*—people in their late teens and twenties—grew up with the Internet, mobile phones and video games. They barely watch TV, hardly ever read a newspaper or listen to the radio, and spend most of their waking hours on the Internet and their mobile phones with ambient media, usually music of their choosing, piped from their PC speakers or an iPod.

In an interview in the *Financial Times* on February 5, 2006, Jim Stengel, the head of marketing for Procter & Gamble, the world's biggest advertiser with a budget of $6 billion a year, described the erosion of Procter & Gamble's ability to reach consumers through 30-second television commercials. Twenty years ago, "television networks gathered giant audiences and advertisers carpet bombed them," Stengel told the *FT*.

"But the couch potatoes acquired defense mechanisms," the *FT* continued. "The first stirrings of resistance came in the 1980s when the spread of television remote controls enabled viewers to take breaks from the commercials. It could be said that a new breed of Homo sapiens evolved with the temporal parameters of the commercial break hotwired into their nervous systems. The rules of engagement turned against advertisers more decisively this decade." Digital video recorders allowed viewers to fast-forward past television commercials. The rise of the Internet and the growing number of cable channels gave viewers alternatives to network fare. And, just as worryingly, younger people seemed to be using several entertainment devices at once. Advertisers face the prospect of paying to reach viewers who aren't watching TV.

If old media grasped the cosmic shift that their audience is making, why would TV advertising revenues be rising as viewership declines? Because TV advertisers are frightened.

The Stanford Institute for the Quantitative Study of Society reported in January 2005 that "the average Internet user spends three hours a day online, almost double the 1.7 hours the average respondent spends watching television." The report adds that the typical Internet user watches television 30 minutes less per day than he or she did in 1995, before the Internet came on the scene. However, spending on network TV advertising has nearly doubled during the past 10 years to $22.8 billion per year, while spending on cable TV advertising has nearly tripled to $15.9 billion over the same period. The rise in spending on advertising to chase a diminishing audience makes no sense in a rational model, but does make sense in an emotionally driven model, where the principal emotion is fear. Advertisers to young people are afraid, and this makes them good candidates for buying billboards on new media; and communities represent new media.

What's wrong with this picture? We're watching giant corporations with experts in advertising throw good money after bad. They are chasing the will-o-the-wisp millennial who TiVos through the ads on TV—when she watches, which isn't often—and spends most hours on her mobile phone, Internet, iPod, DVD or all of them at once.

Stengel continues, "For big companies, the numbers grew increasingly forbidding. As recently as the 1980s, when there were still only two commercial channels in the UK, P&G reckoned it could reach 90 percent of the country's consumers with just three television advertisements. Now it reckons it would take more than 1,000 to have the same impact."

Stengel said in a recent speech to the American Association of Advertisers, "We must accept the fact that there is no 'mass' in 'mass media' anymore." (Gary Silverman, "How May I Help You?," *Financial Times*, February 5, 2006, p. W1). He did not address the issue of P&G's strategies to find the new consumers. Therein lies the new paradigm. Will P&G be a colonist in cyberspace? Or will P&G continue throwing good money after bad?

Well, Mr. Stengel, have no fear. In Chapter 8 I have designed a social network business model for one of your products.

User-Generated Ads

The millennials are literally taking control of the source and type of their media. Many of the big consumer product and service companies will face extinction if they don't get a grip on how best to reach the millennials. Investment banks and tuned-in management consultants are telling them to adopt the user-generated business model using a cooperation-based community platform or else take their golden parachutes and be gone—let the 20-somethings run the show. A friend of mine who is an investment banker in the media and communications industry told me back in November 2005, "We are telling all of our clients that they have five years left, if they do not change their business models now."

The Economist reported in April 2006 that a survey by Online Publishers Association found that 69 percent of America's Internet users have watched video on the Web; 24 percent watch at least once a week and 5 percent do it daily.

In another article from the *Financial Times*, the late Gary Betty, for many years the CEO of EarthLink, came to the realization that traditional advertisements attract criticism. "On Valentine's Day, Mr. Betty announced that EarthLink would stop using its own adverts and run a contest for the best user-generated advert submitted to the *Daily Source Code* and other PodShow podcasts carrying its advertising" (Aline van Duyn, "Whose Space? How Advertisers Are Struggling to Fathom Web-wise Teens," *Financial Times*, May 24, 2006, p. 9). With no financial reward available, EarthLink has developed a new method of advertising: having consumers and users create its advertisements, at no cost to the company. EarthLink has 4 million subscribers whom it has treated well for 10 years and who are loyal to the brand. Sky Dayton, EarthLink's founder, has won their trust, and he knows how to build on it.

Chevrolet tried the user-generated advertising strategy in March 2006, to its chagrin. According to the *Wall Street Journal* on April 4, 2006. "Chevrolet introduced a Web site allowing visitors to take existing video clips and music, insert their own words and create a 30-second commercial for the 2007 Chevrolet Tahoe." Most of the ads created by readers of the blog attacked the Tahoe for consuming excessive amounts of the planet's oil. A typical user-generated ad read, "Our planet's oil is almost gone. You don't need G.P.S. to see where this road leads." Like other consumer product giants, Chevrolet was so anxious to show it was "with the program" by seeking user-generated ads that it forgot to create a community first. What's the oldest adage in business? "Make friends before you make funds." The people who run marketing at Chevrolet apparently never learned it.

Other consumer-oriented corporations have recently created online communities with better success than Chevrolet, yet with not much to write home about. Carnival Cruise Lines created CarnivalConnections .com in early 2006 to make it easy for cruise fans to encourage others to join them, compare destinations and comment on onboard entertainment. The site has attracted 13,000 visitors, according to Diana Rodriguez-Velasquez, director of Internet and database marketing at the company. To encourage young soccer players to post their own photos, blogs and video clips, Nike created Joga.com (*joga* means "play" in Portuguese) and by May 2006 had attracted 2,835 member profiles linked to Portugal's Cristiano Ronaldo, a Nike endorser.

Kellogg began an invitation-only site for women interested in losing weight called skspeak.com and it has attracted 1,000 members. Coca-Cola created a site that enables visitors to create ringtones, but the ringtones work on only three phone models, and there are 160 in all. It needs more work.

Nissan owner Michael Andes of Gaithersburg, Maryland, created NissanClub.com, where its handful of members trade pictures, find parts and gossip about upcoming designs. When asked why Nissan has not launched its own online community, Stephen Kerho, director of interactive marketing for Nissan North America, said, "When you try to corporatize these consumer-generated sites, it's not very credible" ("Their Space.com," *Forbes*, May 10, 2006, p. 124). Ah, but it can be done, and done well, Mr. Kerho.

I agree that it's not very credible if it's started and run by Nissan employees, but a facilities management contract given to an online community management company, like OneSite.com, could solve that problem. Communiteers are much better positioned at launching communities than are old corporations. Control has transferred to the millennials, and the millennials are the Diogeneses who will lead the old corporations into the age of communities.

In Chapter 15 I describe a community called Mocketeering.com that will bring together the wisdom of mobs of people who like to write ads for giant corporations. If the corporations agree to pay for the best ads, it will certainly enhance their credibility. It will be a start.

Advice to Corporate Community Launchers

I can imagine the directors of business development at large corporations around the globe getting pretty fed up with my book at about this point. I have said some things that do not bode well for their chances of launching successful online and mobile communities. The biggest obstacle they have to overcome is distrust: The marketplace for their goods or services often does not believe them, and therefore they cannot launch communities to which users come in order to learn about the corporations' products and services. But here is what large corporations can do that borrows on the concept of online and mobile communities.

- Launch products experientially and make the experience of finding the "hidden" new product one that people who search for the new product will want to share, and they will share it on the corporation's online community.

- Place your products in online games as Jeep has done with Lara Croft Tomb Raider and Diet Sprite has done with Splinter Cell Chaos Theory. Today there are 132 million teen and adult gamers in the United States, where nearly half of all households have a game console. Marketers are desperate to engage this well-to-do audience, according to a July 24, 2006, article in *Forbes* magazine. The video game makers, such as Electronic Arts, need the cash, because each game costs around $20 million to develop. Procter & Gamble sponsors Danica's Secret 500 Challenge, a racing game in which players can create characters that compete on the track. Toyota Motor Corporation recently created Club Scion, an online hangout in Whyville.com, an interactive community of 1.7 million kids ages 15 and under. Toyota executives are sent updates on numbers of visitors, chat topics and accessories purchased. Toyota also provides Scions for avatars to purchase in SecondLife, a remarkable online community for adults. Spending on in-game advertising and product placement, which was $56 million in 2005, is expected to reach $730 million by 2010, according to the Yankee Group, a Boston, Massachusetts, research firm.
- There will be hundreds of thousands of communities launched in the next three years, including 2007. If I were a business development officer of a large corporation, one of several things I would do is build a business model of the online or mobile community that would be of the greatest benefit to my corporation, then find the entrepreneurs to launch it and make a venture capital investment in their company. In that way, I will have an ownership stake, through my shares, in a burgeoning online or mobile community, and I can make discrete references to the corporate mantra, place ads appropriately and block out ads of competitors. Chicago-based Optit.com develops communities for corporations.
- Online marketing is no longer about ad impressions—numbers of people who see your advertisement on the Web. It is about *experiences*. You might think of sponsoring experiential events in communities that have no financial or legal relationship with your

corporation. For instance, if a community is launched to enable high school principals to share ideas and data, and if your corporation sells life insurance and annuities, you might offer the users of that community $50,000 in prize money to the three principals who submit the best stories or the best solutions to a problem in schools in exchange for calling it the "John Hancock Life Insurance" prize.

At the Digital Edge

Karell Roxas, 24, a senior editor at gURL.com, begins each day in her Williamsburg, Brooklyn, apartment with a diet of Gmail, Hotmail, work e-mail, NYTimes.com ("I haven't picked up a print newspaper in forever," she says) and blogs, in that order. She says it is a necessary regimen for maintaining a functional dialogue both at work and in her circle of friends ("A Generation Serves Notice," *New York Times*, January 22, 2006, p. B1).

The *New York Times* reported in January 2006 that "Ms. Roxas' daily pattern is in line with recent research from the Pew Institute and American Life Project, which has found that while certain aspects of online life have become common across many age groups, it is the millennials who live at the digital edge.

"Among those with access to the Internet, for instance, e-mail services are as likely to be used by teenagers (89 percent) as by retirees (90 percent), according to Pew researchers. Creating a blog is another matter. Roughly 40 percent of teenage and 20-something Internet users do so, but just 9 percent of 30-somethings. Nearly 80 percent of online teenagers and adults 28 and younger regularly visit blogs, compared with just 30 percent of adults 29 to 40. About 44 percent of that older group sends text messages by cell phone, compared with 60 percent of the younger group." A *blog*, or Web log, is the newest means of broadcasting ones thoughts and ideas to the world, and since blog messages are sent directly from PC to PC, to PDA, they travel via a P2P network.

The sources of information that power into Karell Roxas' brain are indicative of what is happening with new members of the workplace and their technology. But in the age group 6 to 12, children are playing video games and joining communities as a means of "experiencing" life. Highlights from the National Speak Up 2005 data findings are shown in the sidebar. Figure 3.1 gives an overview of the participants. (More information is available at http://www.netday.org/SPEAKUP/pdfs/NetDay_2005_Highlights.pdf.)

PARTICIPATION OVERVIEW

Geography: All 50 states, DC, Puerto Rico, Guam, and Department of Defense schools world wide

Top 10 states: TX, CA, IL, MD, PA, AZ, MO, NC, CO, MA

Major cities: Baltimore, Chicago, Denver, Houston

Total Participation: 185,000 students, 15,000 teachers, 2,082 schools

STUDENTS	TEACHERS
Grade Distribution • K–2 (11%) • 3–5 (30%) • 6–8 (33%) • 9–12 (26%) **Gender Distribution** • Female (50%) • Male (50%) **School Characteristics** • Public (89%) • Private (11%) • Urban (38%) • Suburban (35%) • Rural (28%) • Title I eligible (44%) • Majority Minority Population (36%)	**Grade Assignment** • K–5 (34%) • Gr. 6–8 (22%) • Gr. 9–12 (27%) **Gender Distribution** • Female (80%) • Male (20%) **Age Distribution** • under 29 (15%) • 30–39 (24%) • 40–49 (27%) • 50+ (33%) **Teaching Experience** • 1–3 yrs (14%) • 4–10 yrs (31%) • 11–15 yrs (16%) • 16+ yrs (39%)

FIGURE 3.1   NetDay 2005 Speak Up Event Participation Overview

---

Selected Student Highlights

Tech Devices and Tools

- The cell phone is the students' favorite communications tool.
- About 65 percent of students in grades 6 through 12 use e-mail and/or instant messenger every day.
- Personal web site use (like MySpace.com) tripled from 2004 to 2005—by grade 12 almost 50 percent of students report personal web site use on a weekly basis in 2005.

Tech Activities—In and Out of School

- Students' number one use of the Internet is research for assignments—but creating a slide show, movie or web page is a strong number two this year—with special intensity for middle school students.
- Video and online gaming continues as a favorite activity outside of school. About 79 percent of students play video games and say the appeal is the "winning" and the "strategy of the game."

Student Ideas about Tech Use at School

- "What if you were designing a new school for kids just like you?" The number one tech request from students in grades K–12: laptops that every student can take home.
- Students believe that good tech skills are necessary for success in school, in college and for a job.

Trends to Watch

- Almost 50 percent of students in grades 6–12 are positive about the value of online learning.
- On average, 17 percent of students nationally declare an interest in a career in the tech industry, but this number varies depending on the geographic area of the country.
- Students say they want to "experience" science—field trips, simulations, real-world problem solving.

(*Source:* http://www.netday.org/SPEAKUP/)

Control is transferring from teachers to 6th to 12th grade students, almost half of whom want to learn online. Yet in the same study it is shown that fewer teachers are as technologically astute as their students. Plus, they are more controlling. When asked what they want most, most of them answered "fast, wireless Internet access throughout the school." The students' answer to the same question was "laptops that every student can take home."

It appears that control is transferring in schools from an 8:00 A.M. to 3:00 P.M., four walls, students sitting in rows at desks with pencils and notebooks type of education, to an online, experiential form of education with Internet, Web and community access. Wherever there is change on this scale, entrepreneurs rush in to capitalize on the change. It is happening in biodiesel fuels; it is happening in media; it is happening in telephony with VoIP, wireless and Wi-Fi disrupting conventional telecommunications; and it is happening in the military with video war games replacing traditional forms of instruction.

Neoteny Will Triumph

Neoteny is a zoological term that means the retention of juvenile features in the adult organism. With younger people receiving their information from trusted friends (or strangers) in their online and mobile social groups and via the Internet and Wi-Fi in coffee shops, and with a constant flow of younger people adopting these habits and gaining purchasing power, the conversation that we call consumer markets will change dramatically.

The endorsers of products and services, from cough syrup to travel to the Czech Republic, will shift from their producers or advertising agencies to communiteer-founded and operated associations, guilds and a form of *Consumer Reports* that embeds RFID tags onto consumer products. Prior to buying over-the-counter allergy medicine at the drug store, we will text-message via our cell phones to a reputation management service to which we subscribe to obtain recent opinions on the various brands that line the shelves.

This disruption in the consumer marketing channel will be huge, fostering a handful of billion-dollar corporate wipeouts and thousands of megamillion-dollar entrepreneurial opportunities. This disruption will force brand owners to slash their advertising budgets for their allergy medicines, cough syrups and thousands of other products, from aspirin to weed whackers, thus depriving television and print media of tens of billions of dollars in ads. In fact, advertising agencies will merge or go out of business, leaving but a handful to handle major events such as the Super Bowl, March Madness and the Academy Awards. Advertising will play a very small role in the age of communities. The wisdom of crowds will replace it. And crowds are genetically wired to share their wisdom with others. The revolution will find communiteers standing on top of the *bastides*.

The Disruption of Telephony Monopolists

Picture this: You are the CEO of a major switch-based telephone company that has provided local and long distance phone calls for more than 100 years to the citizens of your country for a fee per call, based on time and distance. You never got into wireless. Along comes voice over Internet protocol (VoIP), which makes all phone calls free or else packaged in with your monthly Internet service provider (ISP) fee. Calls are free or nearly free on Skype, a P2P VoIP network, and with eBay's capital fueling its growth, Skype will doubtless force the ISPs and telecoms to charge less and less for VoIP phone calls. Any way you look at it, switch-based telephony has been completely disrupted by VoIP.

Let's call your telephone company Monopoly Telecom, and let's assume that most of your senior managers, like yourself, worked their way up from pole-climbing, or maintenance or engineering, without ever needing to, or learning how to, compete with an alternative service. Your business skills are not in the category marked "how to compete" because your business experience has been solely within a monopolistic organization. You see your revenues decline, as Qwest's have done, as your subscriber base shifts to VoIP. France Telecom laid off 17,000 employees in February 2006. AT&T laid off 20,000 workers in March 2006. Your company could be next to vanish. Consultants are called in and they tell you that you will soon be in the real estate business. You weep into your pillow at night.

"The real estate business?" you demand the next morning, after reading your Promethean severance package, your veins bulging in your too-tight Armani shirt collar. "Yes," they respond. "Change your business model fast, or die at the helm of your ship," the consultants say. You challenge them to explain this statement, and they respond: "Monopoly Telecom has 100,000 employees and 35 switches, each occupying a square block of prime real estate throughout the country. The 100,000 employees watch the switches 24 hours a day, but soon the switches will no longer be needed. You will be selling the land and buildings that house them to developers if you move fast."

"What do you mean if I move fast?" you demand.

"Retail commercial space is moving to the Internet, so retailers won't want your downtown locations that used to once house switches. High-rise apartments in downtown locations will not be in demand for long as people telecommute from their country homes. Industrial production is shifting to cheaper markets, such as China, South Korea, Ireland and so forth. Who will want your 35 square blocks of formerly prime downtown space? That will be one of your two big challenges," the consultant says.

"What's the other?" you ask, chewing on a tear-soaked handkerchief.

"Paying severance to the 100,000 people you will be laying off," the consultant says, as he asks for his check and then leaves the boardroom, texting to his partner that the meeting went well.

This snapshot of the next five years of the switch-based telecommunications industry is the breeding ground of several new billion-dollar entrepreneurial opportunities. They include creating socially useful downtown parks and other spaces serving the public good. Across Meridian Street from the world-renowned Indianapolis Children's Museum is an abandoned building housing an old telephone switching station. The name "Indiana Bell" has been rubbed off the brick façade, but it still shows through. If it were knocked down, a park could be built that would welcome back the birds and flora that once inhabited this corner, thus providing a lesson in biodiversity for the children who visit the museum. Other businesses that will rise with telecom's decimation include training and outsourcing former telecom industry employees, and selling old switches to third world countries, old bricks to builders and old real estate in prime locations to creative buyers. The used copper wiring that made the switches carry our calls can be saved and sold for big bucks. And what about the pension funds of the laid-off telecom employees? The solution for this problem will fall to the workout and turnaround consulting industry.

Other Industries That Will Decline

Telephone companies won't be the only big employers with large numbers of employees and large blocks of real estate to dispose of. Control of the conversation in developed countries will forever shift in the following industries:

Apparel	Home mortgages
Advertising	Law
Automobiles	Life insurance
Automobile insurance	Movies
Carpets	Music
Commercial banking	Mutual funds
Consumer finance	Personal computers
Cosmetics	Personal hygiene products
Home appliances	Travel
Home furnishings	Venture capital

It is not for merry schadenfreude that I predict the decline in relevance and size of the preceding handful of industries over the next three to five years, but rather to make two points. First, the rise in importance of online and mobile communities will decimate a number of older industries, because they will lose their relevance to the markets they used to serve.

Second, you can make yourself a fortune consulting for these industries, and I show you how in Chapter 14.

- *Broadcasting.* The major TV networks and cable channels will lose market share to start-up audience aggregators such as OhmyNews that reward consumers to gather and write news stories. Vinod Baya and John du Pre Gauntt, writing for PricewaterhouseCoopers, argue exactly this in a report entitled "The Rise of Lifestyle Media" (as quoted in *The Economist*, April 20, 2006). Successful media companies, they write, will become members of a "marketplace that lets consumers search, research, share and configure their media experiences." Students at Swarthmore College, on the Pennsylvania main line, formed www.warnewsradio.org, which gathers e-mails and blogs from students and others on the streets of Baghdad. This news often contradicts the administration's "pretty face" war news.

- *Movie distributors.* Americans spend much more on video games than they do on movie tickets. Halo 2 had greater first-week sales than the sixth and final sequel of *Star Wars* did for its total run. On average, Americans devote 75 hours a year to playing video games, much more time than they spend on movies. One game company earns more each year—$3 billion in 2004—than the combined revenues of the top 10 grossing movies. World of Warcraft has 22 million active players. One video game alone, Nintendo's Mario, did $7 billion in revenues lifetime, more than double the revenues of all *Star Wars* movies. All movie sales—theater and DVD—grossed $4 billion in 2005. The U.S. Army's training videos, *America's Army* and *Army Adventure*, have been given away but, had they been sold, would have grossed $600 million. Movie distribution will either have to morph to small and handheld screens controlled by crowds or downsize dramatically.

- *Venture capital.* Online communities can be launched with $300,000 or less capital. Angel capitalists such as my firm, Santa Fe Capital Group, can handle $300,000. Following their launch, most online and mobile communities will be funded with float in the form of subscription fees paid by members either monthly, quarterly or annually, tip jars or fees from strategic alliance partners. Old corporations will pay the communiteering companies up-front royalties to include their products in the communities as product placements and to encourage user-generated ads. Online and mobile communities will represent the majority of company start-ups from 2007 through 2010; mobile communities will receive monthly payments from the carriers for minutes consumed. Venture capitalists will have fewer investment opportunities to consider and will downsize their staff. Float, strategic alliances, angel capital and wireless carrier payments are all less expensive capital than venture capital. See Chapter 6 for more on float.

- *Law.* Watch for the rise of the *pro se* litigators. Lawyers have been obfuscating the tautology of the legal predicaments that their clients face for far too long. Some of them charge exorbitant hourly rates, frighten their clients with worst-case scenarios and stretch out cases and their fees by winking and nodding at the lawyer for the other side, knowing that each can make more money by filing more motions, taking more depositions and refusing to settle. Lawyers have controlled consumers in the same way that telephone companies held their monopoly. In Chapter 25 I lay out a business model for a communiteer to use to capture the multibillion-dollar pro se litigation market and put it into the hands of users.

Summary

- Some grand old Goliaths of the Standard & Poor's and Dow Jones Industrial Average are going to, as the old gospel song goes, "lay down and dieth" at the hands of community mobs.
- Control will transfer to communities between 2007 and 2010, and the sound of grown men weeping into their severance checks will be heard throughout the land.
- The rise of communities and the wealth creation of communiteers and their angel backers and early employees will mark the age of

communities. Media companies are already shrinking. Philip Meyer, in his book *The Vanishing Newspaper*, writes that the last reader will recycle the last newspaper in 2040. Media companies may hang in there a bit longer, if they acquire the best online news and entertainment communities. Many small audiences are as good as one large audience.

- With the transfer of control from producers of goods and services to consumers aggregated into crowds in hundreds of thousands of on-line and mobile communities, disruption will come on a scale that only entrepreneurs and their angel capitalists will love. The Austrian economist Joseph A. Schumpeter, writing in the 1930s, was the first to define the word *entrepreneurs*. He called them "creative de-stroyers." To invert a phrase that baseball fans know well: "Say it is so, Joe."
- The wealth that communiteers will create in the period 2007 to 2010 will approach $1 trillion.
- Because they will rely less on venture capital, communiteers and their employees and angel backers will keep most of the new wealth.

4

The Function of Cooperation

The Semantic Web is not a separate web but an extension of the current one, in which information is given well-defined meaning, better enabling computers and people to work in co-operation.

—Tim Berners-Lee

Public Goods

New modes of communication dictate new ways of operating businesses. The Internet has lowered the cost of communication, enabling anyone to create and sell the subject of his or her conversation via blogs. In fact, it is now possible for more people to pool more resources to solve collective action dilemmas. But isn't that the history of civilization in a nutshell?

There are millions of blogs, but one of them, DailyKos.com, launched by Markos Moulitsas, receives 20 million hits every day. If Alexa ranked blogs with Web sites, DailyKos.com would rank in the top 10 of all web sites. Blogs are reminiscent of pamphleteering, a Revolutionary War era form of pseudonymous political positioning. They are also central to virtual marketing, and a very useful means of bringing early users to your community.

Marc A. Smith, Microsoft's research sociologist and developer of Usenet.com, says, "Collective action dilemmas are the perpetual balancing of self-interest and public goods" (Howard Rheingold, *Smart Mobs*, p. 31). A *public good* is, for example, whales, playgrounds, a lighthouse that the community builds, or the Internet or the Brooklyn Bridge or the Public Broadcasting System. Matt Ridley, an expert in public goods, wrote:

> Big game hunting became the first public good. When our ancestors descended from trees, they found themselves on an African grassland. One of the things grasslands made possible were big game animals. Hunger drove our forebears to coordinate their actions to bring down animals so large that all the meat couldn't be consumed before it spoiled. In those circumstances, everyone in the group was free to eat—even those who did not take the risk of hunting. The meat wouldn't be available in the first place unless a few people mustered the gumption to tackle large creatures, but the benefit of the cooperative activity of a few extended to all, even to those who had not participated in the hunt. (Matt Ridley, *The Origins of Virtue*, pp. 105–106)

At my vineyard north of Santa Fe, New Mexico, water is provided by a ditch, or *acequia*, as it has been called since about 1610. My farm has the right to use the ditch eight hours a week. I belong to an *acequia* association along with 24 other families. We all share the same water. We pay $35 per annum for services, but they do not include cleaning weeds, sand and rubble out of the ditch. I have to do that, as do the other members of the *acequia* association. It is a public good which, along with its association has existed for 400 years without centralized authority.

A public good is a resource from which all may benefit, regardless of whether they help pay for it. If everyone acts in their own self-interest all of the time, then public goods are never created. Because there are numerous public goods from which all of us benefit, it can be assumed that cooperation is something all of us do from time to time for the benefits we derive. Using the primitivism model, the hunter-gatherers provided for all members of their community, and if they ate what they killed, they were shunned and sent packing. Reputation management—or its original name, "gossip"—drives them away. If the *acequia* is not cleaned and weeded every April by the able-bodied men and women whose families share the water, then it is a public good that will be wasted. Public goods, therefore, are created and sustained by the cooperative efforts of everyone involved.

The Tragedy of the Commons

Another problem faced by sharers of a public good is overconsumption. Take, for example, an intersection of two busy streets which is permitted by the community to have four gasoline stations erected on its four corners. The operators will overconsume the common area and destroy each other's profit margins until two or three go out of business, making lines longer and prices higher at the one that survives.

City planners are frequently guilty of permitting overconsumption of the scarcest resources of their community. They favor developers, it seems, and often take jobs with the developers whom they favored when they are voted out of office. Milton Friedman pointed out this phenomenon in 1958 with his thesis that government agencies are regulated by the people and groups they are supposed to regulate because of the revolving job doors between regulators and regulatees. Former Attorney General John Ashcroft became a lobbyist after leaving office and has been successful at bringing contracts with the Homeland Security Department back to his native Missouri. This is one of thousands of examples that prove that centralized authority cannot be trusted to preserve the public good.

The Internet as a Commons

Garrett Hardin wrote an article in 1968 for *Science* magazine, entitled "The Tragedy of the Commons," in which he said:

> The tragedy of the commons develops in this way. Picture a pasture open to all. It is to be expected that each herdsman will try to keep as many cattle as possible on the commons. Such an arrangement may work reasonably satisfactorily for centuries because tribal wars, poaching, and disease keep the numbers of both man and beast well

below the carrying capacity of the land. Finally, however, comes the day of reckoning, that is, the day when the long-desired goal of social stability becomes a reality. At this point, the inherent logic of the commons remorselessly generates tragedy.

As a rational being, each herdsman seeks to maximize his gain. Explicitly or implicitly, more or less consciously, he asks, "What is the utility *to me* of adding one more animal to my herd?" This utility has one negative and one positive component.

1. The positive component is a function of the increment of one animal. Since the herdsman receives all the proceeds from the sale of the additional animal, the positive utility is nearly +1.
2. The negative component is a function of the additional overgrazing created by one more animal. Since, however, the effects of overgrazing are shared by all the herdsmen, the negative utility for any particular decision making herdsman is only a fraction of –1.

Adding together the component partial utilities, the rational herdsman concludes that the only sensible course for him to pursue is to add another animal to his herd. And another. . . . But this is the conclusion reached by each and every rational herdsman sharing a commons. Therein is the tragedy. Each man is locked into a system that compels him to increase his herd without limit—in a world that is limited. Ruin is the destination toward which all men rush, each pursuing his own best interest in a society that believes in the freedom of the commons. Freedom in a commons brings ruin to all.

Public goods become more valuable the more people share them. But managing collective resources comes at a price. There are free riders who take from the commons without paying their fair share, such as subway turnstile jumpers.

The Internet is a commons, a public good. It has in most countries (China is a major exception) avoided centralized authority. The U.S. House of Representatives, in passing the Communications Opportunity, Promotion and Enhancement (COPE) Act of 2006 by a vote of 321 to

101, attempted to regulate the Internet by favoring large telephone companies and permitting them most favored nation status over Internet service providers. More than 300 of our elected officials clearly don't get the obvious: The Internet is a public good.

Unlike the commons on which Hardin's herdsmen graze their animals, the Internet can expand indefinitely by adding routers. Yet there are users of the Internet who continually devise means of destroying its universal utility. These are the hackers, spammers and predators who act like wolves in sheep's clothing, stealing identities, credit cards and the lives of the young and the gullible.

In response to these noncooperators, known in game theory as "defectors," users of the Internet cooperate more aggressively because our primitive aversion to centralized authority kicks in. We join online communities.

Shun the Pike Road

I may be overusing examples from the Hudson Valley, but one of the three legs of the stool on which my hypothesis stands—that we are entering the age of communities—is that the Internet is entering its second stage, and I liken it to the second wave of colonists who came to New Amsterdam from Holland. Some of them grew apples in Duchess County and took the apples over hill and dale by horse-drawn cart to the Hudson River, where they sold them to food wholesalers or swapped them for shovels, cups, saucers, and so on. Seeing the apple-filled carts pass in front of their houses, avaricious landowners in the seventeenth century put pikes on roads that ran in front of their homes, and charged tolls to loaded wagons who sought to pass by. Hence, the word *turnpike* to designate a toll road, because the farmers had to pay a toll in order for the landowner to "turn the pike."

You have probably seen roads named "Shun Pike," which were cut through forests by the farmers who sought to carry their apples and corn to markets without having to pay to turn the pike. Building roads that shunned the pike is like building VoIP networks to make telephone calls free, or buying TiVo to shun TV advertisements.

In the rapidly growing world of massively multiplayer online role-playing games (MMORPG, or "morpeg" for short), which are now played in 100 million households and have exceeded movie box office revenues with 2005 sales of $10 billion, there is no pike to turn. But a canvas with 100 million live players is very tempting to consumer product herdsmen. Gamers joy-stick their way around digital likenesses of New York City, and game developers see dollar signs when consumer product advertisers come calling. What about a Jeep for the game players to drive? And the billboard they pass? What about a Jeep ad? That's what you get in a game called American Wasteland. Jeep's marketing department noted that TV viewers in the actively consuming 18- to 24-year-old age group were shunning its 30-second TV spots, so they asked the owner of the "pike," called American Wasteland, if Jeep ads could appear alongside the pike. A licensing deal was struck.

And rather than bore the gamer with the same product placement day after day, the product can be changed continuously, thus keeping the games fresh. Games makers such as Sony, Activision, Microsoft and Electronic Arts love the additional revenue, just as did Hardin's national herdsmen. But at what point will gamers begin to see negative utility in the product placements and seek out ad-free games? What an opportunity for someone to start a market research firm to measure the effectiveness of product placement ads inserted into online communities. You could become the new ACNielsen in the age of communities—*carpe diem*.

The Prisoner's Dilemma

Why do people cooperate? One thing that impels people to cooperate is the knowledge that they might meet again. If people were absolutely certain that they would never ever meet again, they could treat one another egotistically without fear of repercussion. Cooperative behavior now may increase the chance that, if the people meet again in the future, the behavior will be reciprocated. To optimize reciprocity in future interactions, therefore, people cooperate in the present. Robert Axelrod, perhaps the leading student of cooperative behavior, writes in *The Evolution of Cooperation*:

> What makes it possible for cooperation to emerge is the fact that the players might meet again. . . . It would be best to cooperate with someone who will reciprocate that cooperation in the future, but not with someone whose future behavior will not be very much affected by this interaction. (p. 12)

One of the best marketplaces in which to examine cooperative behavior is the U.S. Senate. In this forum, the 100 members know with absolute certainty that they will interface on many future occasions over a six-year period, and perhaps beyond that. Therefore, they treat each other with courtesy, respect, and in some cases obsequious behavior.

They refer to one another as "distinguished colleague" even though their real feelings may be quite different. Their cooperation takes the form of trading votes. Senator A agrees to give the gift of his vote to Senator B's bill if Senator B will reciprocate with the gift of his vote on some future bill proposed by Senator A. The system works well for the senators but tends to isolate them from the people in other marketplaces with whom they do not interface as frequently or with as much certainty. For example, U.S. senators are not as cooperative with their local constituencies as politicians who are required to stand for election more frequently. Accountability tends to enforce cooperation.

Axelrod attempted to measure the winning strategy for behavior between two people. He invited professional game theorists, sociologists, and mathematicians to submit their favorite strategies for playing the prisoner's dilemma, a simple game in which the solution that a player chooses tells a great deal about the player's willingness to cooperate.

In the prisoner's dilemma, two people who do not know each other and who may or may not ever meet again get off a plane together in an unnamed foreign country to which neither has ever been. They commit a very minor crime together and share the proceeds. The two young people are immediately apprehended by the local police and taken to a jail.

Each is placed in a separate room and interrogated separately. Each is told that the other person is being asked the same questions about the crime and that each has the opportunity to say that the other person is guilty (in which event he will go free) or to admit to the crime in the hope that the other person will also "cooperate" (in which case they both will serve a short sentence). The tendency is to "defect," to claim one's own innocence and implicate the other person. However, the other person could do the same thing. In this instance, both persons serve long sentences.

The prisoner's dilemma is simply an abstract formulation of some very common and very interesting situations in which what is best for each person individually leads to mutual defection, whereas everyone would have been better off if they had mutually cooperated.

Axelrod's experts submitted their favorite strategies for solving the prisoner's dilemma, in competition with one another to see which would be the winning strategy in the long run. The winning strategy was the simplest one, tit for tat. This strategy is the one in which a player cooperates on the first move and then, in the next round, does whatever the other player did on the previous move. Axelrod drew the following conclusions from his contest:

> Surprisingly, there is a single property which distinguishes the relatively high-scoring entries from the relatively low-scoring entries. This is the property of being *nice*, which is to say never being the first to defect.

> Another reason for the success of tit for tat is "its propensity to cooperate after the other player defected." This property Axelrod calls forgiveness with the exception of a single punishment. Therefore, the winning behavioral strategy in an interface between two people (or two groups of people) is:

> *Nice, provocable, forgiving:* This strategy is stable so long as the people who employ it are very clear with the other players that they are employing the tit-for-tat strategy. If they are clear, then the players

will know what to expect in the future. If one then defects, she can expect a provocation, followed by continual cooperation thereafter. If all the members of a community practice this strategy and are clear with one another at the beginning, the level of cooperation in that community will be so outstanding that no other type of behavior will be able to invade it. Therefore, one additional factor must be added to this strategy. That factor is clarity.

Competent communiteers will have the fewest defectors in their communities when they are able to tell each new member upon his or her entry, "I would like you to read this booklet, which sets forth our community's mission and ethical standards. If you can abide by the latter, you will be happy here."

The relevancy of the prisoner's dilemma to users of online communities is that they are not likely to ever meet the other person. Hence, the strong urge to defect. In mobile communities where one of the goals is to meet people physically, there will be fewer defectors.

Modified Version of the Prisoner's Dilemma

Since you will not likely ever be in a real prisoner's dilemma, but you will face numerous choices between cooperating and defecting, let's look at a more realistic game, one that could occur in an online or mobile community where goods and services are traded among perfect strangers. It is a modified version of the prisoner's dilemma and it goes like this.

You are sitting alone in your home one night and the phone rings. The voice is one you have never heard, and you cannot tell if it is male or female, or the age of the caller. The person says to you "If you bring a bag with $5,000 in cash in it at midnight to a place that I will designate, then sit in your car for five minutes out of sight from the place you set down the bag of cash, when you return to the place where you placed the bag of cash, you will see in its place a bag of diamonds worth many times more than $5,000."

You agree to do it, and the exchange goes off exactly as promised.

One week later, the same voice calls you, and makes the same exact offer. You do it a second time—take $5,000 in a bag to the same place, sit in your car for five minutes, then go to the spot where you left the money and retrieve a bag of diamonds worth many times more. You are obviously elated.

A week later, the voice calls you again and repeats the offer. You agree to it, and leave your bag of cash at the designated spot. But when you return to retrieve the bag of diamonds, there is no bag of diamonds awaiting you. You drive home discouraged.

A week later, the voice calls you again and repeats the offer. What do you do?

Game theorists would instruct you to do the following: You tell the voice to leave the diamonds first, go to his car and wait five minutes and you will leave a bag of cash with $5,000 in it if he leaves the bag of diamonds first. That solution is known as tit for tat. It means cooperate as long as the other person cooperates, but defect and continue defecting, if the other person defects, until the other person resumes cooperating.

These games are instructive if you intend to form an online or mobile community, because in most instances the players will be pseudonymous. They can hide behind a pseudonym. In mobile communities, the caller's number gives away her identity. Mobile communities are frequently created to enable and encourage members to meet. Loopt, a mobile phone–based, opt-in social network that sells through Sprint's Boost service, provides a facility for friends to meet and do things together. The revenue model is ads, twofers, discounts and coupons pushed to the members who opt-in to receive them.

In the prisoner's dilemma and in the modified prisoner's dilemma, the players are unknown to each other and will never see each other again after making their decision to cooperate or defect. In other words, in online communities there will always be cheaters.

What form will defection take in online communities? A pseudonymous member/defector will be an employee of a consumer products or services corporation attempting to promote the product or service with hidden messages pushing his brands. In communities formed for teenagers, a defector will be a pervert attempting to meet and injure young people. In communities formed for their members to buy and sell products, a defector will be someone attempting to sell counterfeit products, or take money without sending the product purchased, or receive the product without sending money. It will be your task to root out defectors, and I will give you some assistance with methods for doing that in Chapter 9.

Or Maybe I'm All Wet

I could be completely wrong in predicting a high defection rate in online communities. In mobile communities, where people will use location-sensing techniques to physically meet (and receive *unexpected rewards*), the rate of defection will be small.

But perhaps one of the purposes of joining an online community is to get to know people pseudonymously, and then set up physical meetings several months thereafter. Users group meetings would be helpful in setting dates and places for unique events where members will have a reason to physically get together.

Members of SecondLife.com have been known to flirt with one another online and then meet physically for friendship and romance. Wikipedians meet once a year in St. Augustine, Florida, ostensibly to set standards, but perhaps the real goal is to make new friends. It is too soon to tell—the age of communities is too young. But it would not surprise me if online communities become stepping-stones by which people seek out and meet new friends.

The Difficult Task of Building Trust in Online Communities

An adult trusts about 150 people. In other words, on average, every adult has found 150 people whom he or she trusts, according to Duke University sociologist Lynn Smith-Lovin. Teenagers would love to have that big a circle of trusted friends and co-workers, but they haven't lived long enough. That is why they are ripe for social networks. Unlike teenagers, adults are cautious about members of their group of 150, and about new additions to the group, for fear they might violate their trust.

We are hard-wired for detecting injustice. Trust and the detection and punishment of injustice lie at the heart of human society. They are so important that people will actually harm their own short-term interests to punish those they regard as behaving unfairly. For example, in a game developed by Leda Cosmides and John Tooby, of the University of California at Santa Barbara, two people divide a sum of money (say $100). One makes the division and the other accepts or rejects it. If it is rejected, neither player gets any money. On the face of it, even a 99/1 division should be accepted, since the second player will be one dollar better off. In practice, though, few people will accept less than a 70/30 split. They will prefer to punish the divider's greed rather than take a small benefit themselves.

This makes no sense in a one-off transaction, but makes complete sense if the two participants are likely to deal with each other repeatedly. And this, before the agricultural revolution in the sixteenth century, when fiefdoms fell, was the normal state of affairs. The people an individual dealt with routinely would have been members of his circle of 150 or so friends. Strangers would have been admitted to this circle only after prolonged vetting. Such bonds of trust, described by Matt Ridley, a science writer, as "the origins of virtue" in his book of that name, underlie the exchange of goods and services that are the basis of economics.

Once again the tug of primitivism is at work. Where do teens go to collect 150 friends? They're too young to have many circles that spawn circles that spawn other circles. We know from Howard Rheingold's groundbreaking book *Smart Mobs* that teens build their circles of friends in a unique and clever way.

> Smart mobs consist of people who are able to act in concert even if they don't know each other. The people who make up smart mobs cooperate in ways never before possible because they carry devices that possess both communication and computing capabilities.

Teens desperately want to be included in groups, and the plural is important: *groups*, not group. Rheingold writes of teenagers walking through the brightly lit streets of Tokyo with a group of their friends, holding mobile phones, text-messaging and chatting simultaneously. They are in four groups at once: Tokyo mobs, their group of friends, the person or persons they are texting and the person or persons they are talking to on their phones; or perhaps a fifth group, if they are watching a concert or movie on their mobile phones. On the Internet they are rewarded with many social networks designed to serve their needs—appearance, taste in music, movies and cultural miscellany. Some of the better known online communities for young people are Classmates.com, Xanga.com, Tagged.com, Friendster.com, MocoSpace.com, Facebook .com, MySpace.com, YouTube.com and one called TagWorld.com that helps people build communities in cyberspace. In these online sites, a circle of 150 associates expands exponentially.

Who Are the Trusted?

How did these communities gain the trust of tens of millions of young people? The first and perhaps most important explanation is that young entrepreneurs create the communities, and rookies are considered naïve, primitive and too much like the users themselves to ever violate their trust. Old corporations—even corporations that are highly respected by consumers—cannot create trust-based online or mobile communities without, in my opinion, joint-venturing with online communities. Look at all the failed examples. The potential members fear that their names will be sliced, diced, sold, leased, rented and data-mined to a fare-thee-well. And they are probably right about that.

The second explanation of why start-ups can create trust among their members is that the users are listened to. The wisdom of crowds is respected by start-up communiteers, because the users know that the entrepreneurs who launched the community probably cannot afford market research and marketing experts to design the events and games offered on the community's home page. Naiveté and primitivism win out over slickness. The design of a community should be long on simplicity and short on words. Art is more trustworthy than text. One of the geniuses behind the huge success of Baidu, China's search engine which ranks number four on Alexa, is surely the person who insisted on Baidu having a sparse home page.

The third reason is there is no subscription fee or paid advertising in most online communities. The users are welcomed in to share their experiences, videos, photos, stories and desire to join with similar souls. Experiential marketing is the key to encouraging people to join an online or mobile community. "Come in and share your experiences, your stories, your biographies, your ideas and your intellect and tell six of your friends to do the same, because this community is massive." It's pretty much the same pitch that Rotary Club members make to new businesspersons when they come to town.

And finally, the fourth reason is that the communities' founders do not data-mine or rent the e-mail addresses of their members. They need to build millions of users, and then devise revenue models, while maintaining the bond they have built with users. Old media is clamoring to own online communities, and old consumer products and service companies are searching for ways to do product placements on online communities. But advertising and excessive product placement will result in the tragedy of the commons for all parties. I put this question to the wisdom of crowds: In its eagerness to monetize MySpace, will News Corporation kill the goose that lays the golden eggs?

The Phenomenon Known as MySpace.com

As if overnight, MySpace has become an Internet phenomenon. Launched in January 2004 on a shoestring budget, it now claims more than 110 million registered profiles, about half of which belong to regular users. An estimated 15 percent belong to parents who want to keep an eye on what their children are doing and seeing. According to Nielsen/NetRatings, in July 2006 there were 54.5 million unique visitors. Each day, 225,000 new members sign up, creating their own pages, filling out profiles, uploading photos, and linking to an extended network of like-minded teenagers. The average MySpace user spends over two hours a month on the site.

What's more startling is the way MySpace has already acquired a potent social currency. It is a taste-making force in music, fashion, and other cultural ephemera and a de facto dating service that generates more carnal energy than Match.com on its best days. And in the way that Google, Craigslist and eBay have changed how people share and absorb information and goods, MySpace has changed how people, particularly young people (35 percent of users are under 18), share and absorb one another. They blog, flirt, and diarize; post pictures, videos, personal artwork, songs and poetry; and generously distribute compliments and insults.

In an article in *Vanity Fair* in March 2006, James Verini wrote, "MySpace provides a 'sense of place,' a reality TV show for its subscribers. It is a stage. It is a confessional. It is a kiva where the community comes together to swap stories. And it was acquired by News Corporation for $592 million, 20 months after it was launched." News Corporation paid $54 per member. Of course, some of these members are parents checking in on their children.

"With its infinitely customizable profile pages, like interactive head shots in some central-casting department of life, MySpace has become essential to its users' notions of themselves and their tribes. It is where they concoct alternative personas and download new friends, most of whom they know only online, like so many new MP3s or JPEGs."

MySpace as a Public Good

Teenagers are beginning to delete their profiles from MySpace because of the defectors whom they call "pervs," psychopaths who lure unsuspecting girls and boys into physical meetings to injure them. One teenage girl, named Morgan, age 17, from Sparta, New Jersey, told *CosmoGirl!*:

> I was addicted to MySpace. Every day after school, I'd head straight for my computer instead of doing my homework—my grades even fell. I updated my pictures all the time, had the cool features, and if I didn't get a new comment or friend request every day, it ruined my mood. Then I heard about girls getting raped by people they met on MySpace, and that scared me. So little by little I stopped using it and finally I just deleted my profile. ("Space Age," *CosmoGirl!*, August 2006, p. 104)

MySpace doesn't charge a subscription fee. Rather, its revenue comes from ads. Google, which recently guaranteed MySpace $900 million in revenues from ads over three years, runs ads next to relevant profile phrases on MySpace, as it does on other Web sites, and shares the revenues from click-throughs with Google. This strategic alliance is smart and unobtrusive, because Google is still quite primitive, geekish, a rookie (but a smart rookie). MySpace is a "commons," a public good. If News Corporation overgrazes it with ads for its TV shows, it could lose its audience. It also faces a risk from defectors who prey on teenage girls and boys. How does the owner of a community root out dangerous and sick defectors who can change their pseudonymous personalities frequently? By pattern matching, mining for key words and phrases and refusing admission to suspicious characters. And by reputation management, as Xanga does.

Xanga, a MySpace look-alike, has instituted a rating system where users rank the adult-content level on their and on other blogs. Xanga members cannot see "Ex" (for "explicit") content unless they prove they are 18 by registering with a credit card or faxing some other form of identification. Users can also flag content on other blogs that, for example, use underage nudity. Xanga told the *Wall Street Journal* that as of July 11, 2006, users had submitted 109,978 ratings and 42,235 flags. In my opinion, Xanga is doing something brilliant and important: having its members form posses to drive the bad guys out of Dodge. Good for you, Xanga. You understand the importance of reputation management.

Why People Will Pay Fees in Order to Share

Xanga management understands the message of Hardin. And so we return to Hardin, whose tragedy of the commons began a debate that continues to the present: In the face of the temptation to better oneself, why do we cooperate?

The dilemma posed by Hardin is central to the Hamilton versus Jefferson tug-of-war that created the U.S. Constitution. Alexander Hamilton disdained absolute freedom and saw the need for greater centralized authority to regulate those freedoms. Thomas Jefferson was opposed to a centralized authority in the form of a permanent constitution and believed that people would by their nature cooperate to achieve and sustain public goods. Jefferson drew his intellectual support from John Locke, among others; Hamilton from Thomas Hobbes, who wrote in *Leviathan* that a coercive authority was necessary to regulate society.

"If it moves, tax it," is the war cry of many politicians. There are more than 600 professions in the United States that are taxed—in other words, politicians have placed pikes in 600 highways in order to provide them with the capital to run our governments and meddle in our markets. The form of taxation is the requirement of members of these professions to recertify their membership in the profession each year. Cosmetologists, for example, have to pay a fee to their states to renew their license to cut, color and curl hair. Real estate brokers, attorneys and social workers have to do the same.

If you catch my drift, I am driving you to think about jumping into old markets and becoming the dominant communiteer, then becoming the standard-setter of the new markets, and, by publishing all the news of these markets, including rooting out the troublemakers and free riders, thus become the reputation manager of the community. It is not a new model, as I have said. The Kiwanis and Rotary Clubs of America have done incredible amounts of community service over the years. They stand as a shield against government hegemony over free markets. For it is government officials who take on the role of policeman, gossip collector, rules setter and town crier if civilians fail to act. The communiteers—the entrepreneurial team that creates and manages the community—is the defacto centralized authority for its members. Reflect on the millions of bowlers, softball players, golfers and tennis players, who cooperate by obeying the time-honored rules of our games, and we do so without a centralized authority.

The members will pay you for the benefits you offer. These must include information that has value to them, the right to share information with others with whom they share a commons, the ability to shun the pike put up by the common enemy, the assurance that you will keep out turnstile jumpers through reputation management, and the knowledge that unwanted pervs will be kept out. If the community is formed on a platform of trust, and if that trust is never broken by purposeless fees or inappropriate ads, then users will pay for experiences, games, the right to tell stories, the opportunity to reinvent themselves and the knowledge that they have a *place* online where they are welcomed by friends and colleagues each time they click on.

Reputation Management

The courts work well in the off-line world to dispense justice. But we are colonizing a new ecosystem. How about a new system for dispensing justice in that ecosystem—one without lawyers. Meet me in Chapter 10 for my idea for a business just waiting to happen: The Metaverse Arbitration Association.

Before the Internet began to disrupt economies, cooperation was not the prime mover of goods and services; competition was. In fact, in off-line corporate America, cooperation is often punished by antitrust laws. These laws have not been dragged into online economies, where cooperation is taking a foothold. Heretofore, corporate and government whistle-blowers have not been garlanded in roses when they point out the lies and cheating of their bosses. Whistle-blowers are heroes in online communities. Small groups historically have cooperated better than large groups; but whenever the members of a group cooperate it is because the group has a reputation manager.

eBay invented online reputation management. If you want to succeed like eBay, you must reputation-manage. Why do we send $600 to a perfect stranger, whose "handle" we know because she is on eBay, to buy the collectible that she no longer wants, but we do? We have never met her. We have no reason to believe that she will ship us the collectible, but we send her the money anyhow. The reason that we are willing to pay a large sum of money to a perfect stranger is that eBay offers a reputation manager service. It provides trustworthiness scores for sellers and buyers. If a seller regularly delivers the goods that he promises he will, then the people to whom he sells provide a rating as to the seller's trustworthiness. A rating above 99 percent is very valuable. A rating of 95 percent or below is death to the seller.

There is nothing new, not even in the world of eBay, in the value of maintaining a good reputation in business. Women entrepreneurs have known for years that venture capitalists are loathe to back them because they "don't act like men," and for other reasons. Thus women have consistently launched trust-based businesses in which their capital was provided largely by float—asking the customer or the franchisee to pay their money before the goods or services were provided. In my book *Enterprising Women: Lessons from 100 of the Greatest Entrepreneurs of Our Day*, I found that roughly one-half of America's most successful women entrepreneurs started trust-based businesses. These included Mary Kay Ash, Lillian Vernon, Jean Nidetch and Gertrude Boyle, among others who collectively created more than $10 billion in wealth without raising a plug nickel in venture capital. You bet they knew their reputation was on the line with every customer they dealt with. When your revenues are your capital, maintaining your reputation is vital.

In the history of civilization, defectors have been punished in many ways. Gossip has driven communities to hang, stone, burn at the stake and imprison supposed defectors. Centralized authorities, in the form of governments, judicial systems, militias and police forces, have punished defectors in various degrees of cruel and degrading means. There is no judicial system in the world inhabited by online communities, although I propose that creating one would probably be a wonderful entrepreneurial endeavor.

The logic of game theorists who have studied the prisoner's dilemma persuade me that the opportunities for defecting in online communities are quite tempting, particularly in those created for relatively young and naïve members. And because no one in the free world, except for a handful of politicians, wants to form a centralized authority to govern commerce on the Internet, it is up to the communities to self-govern. Again, the need is most severe where sexual predators prey on the young and the naïve, but the tragedy of the commons forecasts that all public goods risk coming to a tragic end without reputation management.

Publishing the names of betrayers and defectors is the best way to deal with the problem. Of course, the betrayers and defectors will assume new identities, and when their new identities are published, they will assume new ones, and so on, ad infinitum. But the ISPs who sold the defectors their e-mail addresses can be named as well, and since their reputations are valuable to them, they will not continue selling an e-mail address to a person who violates the trust that the communities offer to him. Internet service providers should be watchful of selling multiple pseudonyms to the same person. In Chapter 26, I describe a business model for a new reputation management company that will service all of the communities.

In the largest online community, that of massively multiplayer online video games, there has been quite a bit of sophisticated defection, and one lawsuit, brought in a United States District Court, that did not result in a ruling.

The Rise of Games

The largest communities on the Web and on mobile phones, as measured by numbers of active daily participants, are games. Of all games, the largest and fastest-growing type is massively multiplayer online role playing games, or "Morpegs." According to Edward Castronova, the author of *Synthetic Worlds* and an economist at Indiana University, who is also a Morpeg player and a serious student of the genre, it is estimated that there are more than 130 million Morpeg players worldwide and the number is growing at a rate of 10 percent per year.

A Morpeg is an online computer role-playing game in which a large number of players can interact together or against one another in the same game at the same time. A Morpeg follows a client-server model in which players, running the client software, are represented in the game world by an avatar—this is usually a graphical representation of the character they play. Providers, usually the game's publisher, host the persistent worlds these players inhabit. This interaction between a virtual world, always available for play, and an ever-changing, potentially worldwide stream of players characterizes the Morpeg genre.

Once players enter the game world they can engage in a variety of activities with other players, ranging from chat with their friends or guild members to teaming up in order to kill large enemies or to complete complex tasks or quests that are not achievable alone. Killing these enemies (typically referred to as *mobs* by gamers) yields the players experience points (commonly abbreviated as Exp or XP) and equipment or loot such as armor and weapons. Both the experience points (used to "level up" the character or his abilities) and the loot gained from slaying mobs help to improve the character so he can handle fighting in more adverse situations. The people who develop Morpegs are in charge of supervising this virtual world and offering the users a regularly updated set of new activities and enhancements to guarantee a continual interest in the game. They may also employ moderators to help run the game, who often have the power to patrol, enforce punishments, freeze accounts, and so on.

The online games market has attracted more than 12 million players in the United States and over 110 million in foreign countries, principally China, India and South Korea. The average age of a Morpeg player is 24.3. Players are 92.2 percent male.

The Morpeg community has grown so quickly and spread to virtually every country so rapidly that its need for services hasn't caught the attention of many entrepreneurs. Billion-dollar entrepreneurial opportunities exist in several areas in the Morpeg world. The first is the foreign exchange market. A Morpeg player presently can exchange coins of the realm that he has earned in Norrath, the mythical kingdom of EverQuest II, a very popular game, for U.S. currency on IGE. The players and game developers are not thrilled with IGE earning $30 million a year by operating a foreign exchange market. They want to participate in the earnings of a foreign exchange market. You can become the communiteer for this opportunity.

Defectors in the online games world cause serious problems for gamers and steal money from them. A typical example of cheating is when a seller's avatar does not deliver the land to the buyer's avatar, but keeps his synthetic money, and in turn sells it on IGE for real cash.

A Need to Protect the Public Good

Online communities and mobile social networks, particularly those in which there are unexpected rewards, prizes, opportunities to make new friends, and mythical money at their core, will evolve into major industries. The $800 million in annual currency exchanges of mythical currency earned on Morpegs (2004 figure, as cited by Edward Castranova) will be a drop in the bucket 5 to 10 years from now. Day traders in penny stocks will add liquidity to the market, and where there is liquidity, wealth creation and wealth losses will follow. Even when game developers and distributors provide a caveat, as did Mythic Entertainment for players of The Dark Age of Camelot, such as "Playing the Game for commercial, business or income-seeking purposes is strictly prohibited," income seekers will trample that rule as did the cattle grazers in Hardin's tragic commons.

An income seeker who hired inexpensive day laborers in Tijuana to play The Dark Age of Camelot continuously, and converted his mythical currency to U.S. currency on eBay (when it operated a currency exchange), sued Mythic in February 2002 in the U.S. District Court of Southern California when Mythic asked eBay to block the auctions for "unfair business practices" and "interference with prospective economic advantage." The suit was later dropped (see *Play Money* by Julian Dibbell), but there will be others. In order to prevent outside centralized authority from putting up pikes to be turned for a fee and rules that impinge on the public goodness of the Internet, the owners of online and mobile communities, with the active involvement of their users, must find a way to self-regulate.

Golfers did it. I am part of this happy group of people who chase a little round ball around pasture land, and I can attest to the pleasure and joy of the game and its elevation to spirituality at times, on certain majestic courses and at certain times of the day, made possible by a set of rules adopted 150 years ago in Scotland. The first golfers were drinkers, thrown out of their homes by their wives after dinner because of their rowdiness. In the summer in Scotland, it stays light until 10:30 P.M. It is said by the Scottish that golf has 18 holes because that is how long it takes to finish off a bottle of scotch and still be able to see the flag from besotted eyes at 10:30 P.M. They gave golf its name, legend has it—"Gentlemen Only, Ladies Forbidden"—as a retributive statement for having been sent packing to drink and knock a little ball around with a stick until they staggered home.

If this bunch of drunken rowdies can come up with a set of rules to govern their game, and if those rules can continue to protect the pleasure and camaraderie that gives golf its popularity, then surely developers of online and mobile communities, with their informed, combined intelligence, can do the same today.

Summary

- Online communities are *public goods*.
- Garrett Hardin's "Tragedy of the Commons" predicts that people will inevitably attempt to destroy public goods.
- This is prevented via *reputation management*.
- Mobile communities are less susceptible to defectors because their members know they may meet in real life.
- If online communities encouraged their members to meet in real life at *users groups*, defectors would be less likely to penetrate the public goodness of the communities.
- If a bunch of drunken rowdies, chased out of their homes by their wives, can self-regulate a game of balls and sticks—surely members of online communities can also do it.

5

Appear to Lack Money

What if the wisdom of the crowd were harnessed and its power unleashed, unfettered by outdated intellectual property laws and uninhibited by the dictates of management? The question has many answers. One is that ad agencies had better consider their reason for existing.

—Bob Garfield,
"Inside the New World of Listenomics"

Do Not Appear to Be Succeeding

You can build a community of 20 million happily chatting and paying users, be the strategic partner of choice of the top consumer product and service marketers on the planet, and be deflecting offers of more than $2 billion to sell your company to old media—*and then blow it all by appearing to be successful*. It may seem like reverse logic to you because you have seen rich and famous entrepreneurs buying private jets; getting invited to Allen & Company's annual shindig at Sun Valley, Idaho, for media goliaths; and sporting new homes and vineyards. But that model will not work anymore.

The more liquidity you create in the marketplace, the more you should keep your head under the hood. If you raise venture capital, do not announce it on your web site. Prohibit your investors from doing so as well.

Massive Liquidity

The communities with the greatest liquidity will be worth the most to stockholders or to a potential acquirer. The value of networks increases exponentially as the number of its participants rises. Stated another way, the greater the community mobbing effect, the greater the value of the community to its participants, the owners or an acquirer.

Bebo, a MySpace competitor that had 30 million members as of February 2007, according to *Forbes*, is rumored to be "in play," by possibly Viacom and News Corporation, at an acquisition price above $500 million. I personally would not call Bebo a massively liquid community at 1.7 million, but clearly I am not writing the acquirer's check, either.

The most successful, hence liquid, communities are those with the greatest number of members sending information back and forth. eBay tops the list. If eBay were a country, it would be the eighth largest economy in the world. Internet service providers should form communities because they have the membership base and their base is waiting like a dolphin with its mouth open to be fed. If I ran NetZero or EarthLink, I would jump into the community business with both feet. And I would license the use of my subscribers to mobile content providers and take a cut of the latter's ample revenues.

Internet service providers have subscribers but they do not do anything cooperatively. However, they could be offering broad-based communities such as pet lovers, movies, shopping and journalism as does OhMyNews. Vonage, Skype, VoEX and other VoIP carriers have created liquid networks and should segue to social or business networks as well.

YouTube.com, a start-up community launched a year ago, lets its members upload videos. It already transfers more data each day than the equivalent of the entire Blockbuster video rental chain in one year. AOL has launched AIM.com to compete with YouTube. PutFile.com, a startup in the UK, is competing with YouTube as well. Lulu.com is competing with YouTube.com, and it has boldly gone where YouTube has not: It has asked its users to pay when they upload a video to the community. Will it work? It's too soon to tell. Movie uploading communities have massive liquidity. Both of the founding entrepreneurs of YouTube are centimillionaires with its acquisition by Google for $1.65 billion.

YouTube got its start in San Mateo, California, in February 2005 when Chad Hurley met Steven Chen, a PayPal engineer, at a party. Hurley had designed PayPal's logo in 1999 and was doing some consulting work. They set up shop in Hurley's garage and in May 2005 released a test version of the site, featuring videos of Chen's cat, PJ.

Google was already in the marketplace with its own online video service. YouTube used open source software and wrote its own code. The service can handle 110 video formats and 64 audio formats used by digital photo and video cameras and by mobile phones.

By September 2005, former PayPal chief financial officer Roelof Botha contributed some videos from his honeymoon in Italy on the site. Botha had joined Sequoia Capital as a partner, and he invited Hurley and Chen to present their business case to Sequoia's investment committee. Few venture capital funds have the track record of Sequoia. They funded Apple, Cisco, Yahoo! and Google as start-ups. Sequoia wrote a $8.5 million check for YouTube for a 30 percent equity interest, thanks to Botha.

The number of viewers began to grow virally. Members mobbed the site and by November 2005 YouTube had more than 1 million visitors a day.

Here's where the network effect kicked in: Members of MySpace began using it, and MySpace's owners tried to block their use, which was an endorsement. NBC protested about YouTube's users uploading scenes from *Saturday Night Live* and the Jay Leno show—another endorsement in reverse. It reminded me of Ed Sullivan inviting Elvis Presley onto his Sunday night TV entertainment show in 1956, but only if the camera would shoot him from the hips up. Preachers begged their congregations not to permit their children to listen to rock 'n' roll.

Bill Gates told the *Wall Street Journal* in a July 2006 interview that Microsoft "never could have done what YouTube has because of the copyright issues and the lack of a clear path to profitability." What he may have meant was Microsoft would have been sued because it has deep pockets, but suing YouTube (before Google acquired it) would be a waste of old media's time and money. If YouTube had not announced that it had raised $11.5 million in venture capital, it probably would have never been sued and not been acquired at such an early date by Google. Now, it may not skate across the pond unscathed. I worry that YouTube's founders have not learned about the Chicago bird and that by singing of their successes, they could be attracting litigation.

The Story of the Chicago Bird

Once upon a time there was a bird that lived in Chicago. Each fall as the weather turned colder and colder, the bird would fly South for the winter. But this particular winter, he decided that he was not going to fly South, but save his energy and stick it out in Chicago. So, he sat in his tree as the leaves fell off, the winds began to howl, and the snow began to fall. He wrapped his wings tightly around his body, determined not to fly South. But when it got extremely cold, the bird couldn't take it any longer. So, he lifted off and started to fly South, but the ice on his wings was too heavy and he crashed toward Earth.

"I'm going to die. I'm going to die!" he screamed. But rather than die, he landed on a warm cow pattie and was saved.

"I'm hungry," said the bird. "I'll just eat some of the nutrients in this cow paddy," which he did, and with a full stomach, he began to sing at the top of his lungs about how smart he was.

A wolf heard the little bird singing, and came over and ate him.

The moral of the story is that sometimes we get lucky, and we appear smart. But we all have to eat crap from time to time, along with our lucky and smart events. It is better not to sing out loud about our good fortune, because it could attract predators.

There are lots of times in business when you win by being quiet and lose by talking too much. You mention the people or firms you're doing business with, and the audience may not read the runes like you do, and they might find your partners disreputable and put you in the same category. So what may appear to you as looking smart or lucky may appear to others as eating crap. For instance, if you announce that your new online community has just raised $20 million, you may think you look smart or lucky, but a whole bunch of people know you've just done a dumb thing and raised capital by giving away ownership when you could have generated float instead.

Little Richard's Law

Perhaps by accident, YouTube got mobbed by tens of millions of users as a response to negative publicity, negative buzz, similar to the way that Baptist preachers launched Elvis Presley, Little Richard, Chuck Berry and the other legends of rock 'n' roll. The hell fire and damnation preachers of America launched rock 'n' roll by shouting from the pulpits, "You'll all go to hell, you hip-swivelin' dancers, if you don't change your ways," and thereby made Little Richard famous.

Negative publicity moves faster today then when Elvis was discovered in 1956. People can communicate immediately with friends via blogs, mobile phone calls, SMSing, face-to-face and via computers. I want to repeat for emphasis a sentence from Howard Rheingold's book *Smart Mobs*:

> Smart mobs consist of people who act in concert even if they don't know each other. The people who make up smart mobs cooperate in ways never before possible because they carry devices that possess both communication and computing capabilities.

If we were trying to explain why it is that young people need to be in multiple places at once, now that they have the technological capability to do so, we could stop at Rheingold's dictum, and that would be that.

The equation for Rheingold's Law would read like this:

$$M = P \times C$$

where M stands for mobbed (resulting in millions of members and hundreds of millions of dollars in wealth for the communiteer), P stands for peo-

ple with the desire to join your community, and C stands for the technological capability to do so.

But to distinguish your community from that of every other community seeking to attract the same teenage mobs, we need to add another variable. This variable is N, for negative publicity. By attracting
the ire and outrage of preachers and teachers to your community, you
add the N factor and you will be mobbed a hundredfold more than your
competitor. Little Richard was such an outrageous performer that my
father forbade me to listen to his music or attend his concerts. All the
more reason for me to do it. I love Little Richard for his persona, his
music, and for showing me that risk taking is worth it. The juice is
worth the squeeze. I honor him by naming this new equation in economics after him.

$$\text{Little Richard's Law:} \quad M = P \times C \times N$$

Little Richard's Law states that the rate at which a new community
will be mobbed (M) is equal to the number of people (P) with instantaneous communication capability (C) times the amount of negative publicity (N) churned by established corporations and institutions that are
afraid their ways of doing things will be disrupted. Let's test this equation. Assume that you start a community where advertisements of consumer products and services are mocked by your users, who in turn
contribute their own creative ideas for ads. Call it Mocketeering.com.
You encourage members to join for the purpose of rewriting and improving the advertisements of old traditional corporations, and if the traditional corporations buy a user's ad, the revenues are split 70/30, the user
getting 70 percent and the community getting 30 percent. The wisdom
of crowds instructs us that the ads generated by the crowds who come to
Mocketeering.com will be vastly better than ads written by so-called experts at ad agencies.

The cacophonous, blood-curdling cries of outrage from corporate
America and the advertising community will guarantee you success.
Plus word will spread like wildfire that Mocketeering.com will pay big

bucks for clever ads. See my business model for Mocketeering.com in Chapter 15.

If you start a community that you believe will have disruptive effects on parts of corporate America, be sure that corporate America knows about it. Run press releases on blogs that their corporate bosses are most likely to read. Make them know about you early on. They won't sue you if you always appear to lack money.

Spend time in Salvation Army stores assembling a wardrobe of grungy old clothes and shoes. Do not get haircuts too frequently. Avoid publicity, but if you happen to be photographed, appear underfed and shy. Never, never discuss funding, or capital that you may have raised. If asked about it, answer in this way: "We're member supported."

Barrier to Entry

The purpose of being in business is to make your product or service a substitute for all other products and services, and to make their products and services *no* substitute for yours.

By offering the members of your community every benefit you can conceive of, and permitting them the freedom to create, to fly (the Latin word *competere* comes to mind; it means both to compete and to be able to fly), then you will be putting up barriers to entry in front of potential competitors. I urge you not to seek revenues by selling ads. That's so yesterday. Remember to think primitive: Did the guild halls, Masonic lodges, and meeting halls hang banners for Budweiser, Toyota or Ford tractors on their walls? No, and they still don't. You must gain credibility, and to do so, I recommend that you avoid selling ad space in your community. You can do better than that.

The Primary Sources of Revenue

Float will provide you with most of your revenue. If you require more than $300,000 in capital to launch and operate your site, then you have not provided the most useful potpourri of benefits, and you do not have enough float coming in from members.

The primary sources of revenue for online communities for you to select from are these:

- *Tip jar:* Payments made from the members for the best stories or movies, research, answers to quizzes or photos, with the contributing member receiving 70 percent and the community receiving 30 percent.
- *Kudos:* Payments in scrip that act like tip-jar money but can be used to buy products or services offered in the community, or exchanged at the online foreign exchange market.
- *Reputation management fee:* Publish a monthly newsletter where, among other things, corporate decoys and other invaders are exposed. Charge no more than two dollars a month to begin.
- *Syndication fees:* Sell the best stories, videos and photos to digg.com and other aggregators.
- *Affinity credit card:* Offer your members an affinity credit card with the community's name emblazoned on it. There are numerous fees to be earned with an affinity card, to wit:
  - Loading
  - ATM usage
  - Purchases
  - Money transfers
  - Phone calls
  - Over-limit fee
  - Membership fee
  - Online payment fee
- *Digital rights management (DRM) fee:* Charge nonmembers who have been sent a copyrighted piece of music, video or photo from a member a DRM fee to receive the video, perhaps $2.40 a video, and offer them a free one-year membership to your community.
- *Users group:* Form a users group to encourage members to fill a "suggestion box" with ideas on how to improve the community. Ask the members who want to join the users group to pay a membership fee

of $1.67 per month. Eventually hold a convention for users to meet and implement new revenue sources.

- *Revenue sharing:* For sites such as Mocketeering.com where there is prize money offered to the best ad or movie created by members, share the revenue 70/30 with members.
- *Strategic alliances:* Raise up-front money from old corporations that wish to sit on the windowsill of your company to learn how you might design and operate an online community for them.
- *Facilities management:* Once your community is up and running successfully, offer to launch and manage online communities for your old corporation sponsors under facilities management contracts.
- *Wireless carrier revenues:* Port your content to mobile phones and share the monthly charges with the carriers 50–50 or better.

There are 10 primary and more than 20 secondary fees in the communiteering business. Many of them are float-based. None of them have costs of goods sold. You should make a 40 to 50 percent net profit/revenues ratio in your community and that ratio should grow for at least 10 years, if you manage your business with care. That is an outstanding rate of return. Details on the revenue channels for communities are provided in the business model section, Chapters 9 through 27.

Music and Communities

Little Richard's Law seems to have brought a wonderful outrage against illegal P2P music downloaders like Napster and Grokster. Yet P2P lives on, with DRM as its toll booth. Why won't P2P die? Peer-to-peer platforms owe their popularity to undiscovered musicians. The irony of Little Richard being a musician and P2P surviving a multitude of tirades from the established music industry, yet thriving because of music, is absolutely stunning. Peer-to-peer platform companies are forming to carry the heavy traffic of communities, when server farms, relegated to the horse and buggy age, can't carry the load. But there are such a huge number of independent musicians (called *indies*) strummin' and drummin' on the Web, that P2P has to carry the traffic. The annual number of new releases by musicians grew from 17,000 in 1991 to more than 2 million in 2005. The web site AllRecordLabels.com provides the names of 16,600 labels from 87,000 independent artists in 244 genres, including such narrow categories as Afro-Latin (83 labels), beach (18), bossa nova (72), gay/lesbian (48) and polka (22).

Scooter Scudieri is a successful independent musician without a record label to his credit. He markets his music exclusively over P2P. Scudieri attaches advertising messages to his works and charges his listeners a fee. The ads frequently carry a click-through link to an e-commerce web site. For every click-through, Scudieri is paid a few cents. This singer gets paid up to three ways: for the download, for the ad and for the click-through if it occurs. With more than 50 million searches for his name, Scudieri is the most searched independent artist on the Web. His first video was downloaded more than 250,000 times in 2005.

An indie group in London in 2004 called DNA took Suzanne Vega's song "Tom's Diner," stripped it down, used her vocals and added their own beat to it. Her lawyers (unaware of $M = P \times C \times N$) wanted to sue DNA for copyright infringement. But Vega liked what they did. So she got in touch with DNA, remixed the song, released it, and it became a bigger hit than her 1987 original. In classical economics that is known as *demand pull*. In the language of communiteering it is known as the *network effect*. People listened to the revised version of "Tom's Diner"—pulled it through as it was—and a new, more popular song was born.

Blogging and Viral Marketing

Little Richard's Law kicks in after you have become a popular community. Without customers, a business is not a business. Thus, there is needed a mechanism to attract customers in order to have institutions, corporations and preachers hurl blasphemies at you and your community. You especially want NewYorkTimes.com and CNN.com to report those outrages because of their high Alexa rankings.

Viral marketing is the key. It means to get people chattering about you online. The least costly way to kick-start a mob is by having the top bloggers report about your community. MocoNews, a widely read daily blog published by Rafat Ali, is an important stepping-stone. RCR Wireless (RCRnews.com) is an important daily newsletter for the mobile community world. The DailyKos is another. There are blog collators such as Feedster to help you find the appropriate blogs.

Kevin Rose, a co-founder of digg.com, used Little Richard's Law to great benefit, resulting in massive mobbing and a valuation in a venture capital round of $200 million after a mere 18 months of operations. Approximately 1 million people visit digg.com daily, reading, submitting or "digging" some 4,000 stories. Members can share, upload or vote on articles. Most of the diggers are males in their 20s and 30s and earning $75,000 or more a year.

In July 2006, according to *BusinessWeek*, "AOL tried to lure Digg's top 50 contributors with $1,000 a month to switch to its site, which led Rose to rant on his weekly podcast that . . . Calcanis (a rebuffed, control-seeking angel investor, who subsequently joined AOL) and AOL were trying to squash Digg!" ("Valley Boys," *BusinessWeek*, April 14, 2006, p. 42). Rose's outrage damaged AOL and increased the loyalty of Rose's users to Digg. Now Rose has gathered one of the most desirous demographic groups in the nation to his community.

Firefox aggregated 50 million users in 24 months by blogging to specific audiences. Started by 19-year-old Blake Ross, Firefox makes a new browser that is easier to use than Microsoft or Netscape for blogging. Its customers were so pleased with Firefox that they chipped in money to buy a two-page ad for Firefox in the Sunday *New York Times*. The pitch in the ad was that with each download, the user would receive a free blog. Why is this valuable information for you to have? Because the blog comes from members of the Firefox users community. *Messages from members who share something in common are more valuable to the recipient than are advertisements.*

The rallying support of new believers is the obverse of Little Richard's Law. There is no one as loyal as a convert. The newer the member, the more messianic is his loyalty. The positive benefits of the network effect so outweigh the benefits to the community owner of generating revenues from advertisements, that owners of communities should avoid generating revenues from advertisements at all costs. Messianic members will help the valid community survive. Ad revenues are so old, so yesterday. Moreover, communities started by penniless entrepreneurs are much more trustworthy and will succeed by bringing mobs to share the benefits of the community, and revenues can come—should come—from newer sources. Always show respect for your members. They got you where you are today, and they will be loyal to you all the way to the top, if you respect them completely and unfailingly. JetBlue airlines had to learn this lesson the hard way.

With more than 600,000 indie musicians singing and strumming their hearts out over the Internet to upwards of 250 million finger-tapping listeners, it is time for an entrepreneur to launch the indies equivalent of the Grammys on the Web via an online community in which the attendees are asked to contribute to a tip-jar vote with their dollars. The winners in each category would receive 70 percent of the proceeds and the indies community 30 percent. It would be necessary to set a $10 limit per vote to avoid ballot-stuffing by wealthy fans. A Grammy award show for indie musicians is such an obvious winning community, it will probably be launched in a New York minute.

Will Movies Follow the Path of Music?

Movies require more than 100 megabytes (MB) of storage for a feature-length film. Such a large storage requirement strains the traditional server-client closed-system configuration. It is not a problem for P2P, which "borrows" storage capacity from clients on the network. With P2P software loaded onto a desktop computer, every computer becomes a peer that acts as both client and server. Peer-to-peer technology is extremely efficient because it spreads the workload across many desktop computers, using idle storage capacity and eliminating the need to grab storage from a central server. And during prime time, or for a popular event, P2P permits all of the capacity necessary.

With a DRM pike in the middle of the road, the indie movie distributor can charge a pay-to-play fee, offer a subscription service and capture 15 cents to one dollar or more per click-through. The recipients of the movie can be asked to contribute money to a tip jar for their favorites, thus providing the upstart movie producer 10 cents for every dollar of tips with the community owner keeping 30 cents. These revenues can add up fast. The most frequently visited movie on YouTube.com was an amateur dance video that received over 28 million unique visitors. If 10 percent of them tipped one dollar, the indie producer would have earned $1.96 million. This is your revenue model, YouTube.

The movie industry has a long and established tradition of multi-channel marketing which it calls *windowing*. Windowing means that the theatrical release of a movie is essentially the advertisement for the movie—the means of creating buzz and positive reviews. The buzz then pushes DVD rentals and sales, pay-per-view cable, premium cable, basic cable and broadcast television. Through windowing, the movie's legs are extended, and the talent finds new fans. Peer-to-peer adds another dimension to windowing. Since viewers can be tracked, indies can capture groups that view the movie and send announcements of forthcoming movies that match their tastes. This benefit doubtless will make the P2P channel the number one source of revenues for movies.

Think of the myriad avenues P2P offers the movie producers: viewers commenting on certain events in the movies, viewers doing movie reviews, seeking certain movies to be targeted to schools and museums, fan clubs interviewing the stars, outtakes provided to subscribers, and movies targeted to certain demographics—such as sports and chase movies to the young male market—to achieve premium tip-jar revenues. Director Peter Jackson distributed his diary of clips and outtakes from *Lord of the Rings* via P2P. A director could solicit ideas for a sequel in this manner. Will the major movie distributors see the opportunities spread out on the table in front of them? Or will entrepreneurs seize the day and build digital movie distribution companies that supply the benefits the new demand curve is seeking?

The Oligopolistic Control of the Wireless Network

Given an equally good idea for new communities and equal amounts of capital to fund their launches, Jane and Dick start two new communities. Jane's runs on mobile phones and Dick's runs on the Internet. Which of the two will achieve revenues faster?

Jane's will, of course, because she will have paid a visit to the primary wireless carriers, met their requirements, and they will have charged Jane's users monthly fees for connect time and then paid Jane by check each month 65 percent of the tolls they collect.

Dick's community will launch faster than Jane's, because he would not have been required to obtain approval from and meet the requirements of the wireless carriers. On the Internet, you rent a Web server (about $100 to start), pay for a web site, put your story on it, start a program of virtual marketing through blogs and with search engine optimization (SEO) to find interested users, and you are up and running in 20 days or thereabouts. But you can't ask for subscription fees or introduce other revenue-generating ideas until you have been mobbed by at least 1 million people.

If launching a new community is intensely more revenue generating in the early months, why doesn't every communiteer do a mobile launch rather than an online launch? Why isn't MySpace a mobile community? Why isn't Facebook a mobile community? I think they made a mistake, and by the time it dawns on them to segue over to mobile, competitors may have slammed the door on them.

To launch a mobile community, the first step you will take is to contact an aggregator, and this company will manage your relationships with the cell phone carriers. You will need to have agreements with all of the carriers in order for your service to spread by word of mouth. The aggregator will charge you at least $1,500 a month to begin with. Then you will have to buy a short code, which is roughly equivalent to your web site domain, for about $1,000 a month.

The Somewhat Chaotic World of Mobile Communities

Imagine an accidental invention occurring to Ford Motor Company that suddenly drove millions of people to buy its cars and trucks. Say the invention was the content of news, movies, music and games that issued forth from the dashboards of its vehicles, preprogrammed to the delight and individual tastes of each driver. I would step into my car every morning with a report on PGA news, Tennessee Volunteer football, prices of stocks that I have an interest in, important e-mail messages, and then Ella Fitzgerald singing Cole Porter ambiently as I drove on to work or to a meeting. Something like that might save the beleagured U.S. auto and truck maker, and it is certainly saving the wireless carriers.

They have been thrust into carrying content—news, movies, music and games—without the staff to sort out which content they should carry. The New AT&T, formerly Cingular, employs six people in its content department in Atlanta; Sprint employs five. They are offered hundreds of content choices every month. It's the Coca-Cola bottle problem—a fat middle, but a small mouth. And choosing which content from the middle gets through the mouth is where chaos reigns.

All roads to the carriers lead through Lansing, Michigan. Wireless-Developer Agency (WDA), the brainchild of Konny Zsigo, determines whether or not a mobile game or other mobile content will appear on the decks of North America's wireless carriers. "We receive about 100 submissions per month, and we approve about 30," says Zsigo. Each of the carriers has 150 spaces on their decks, and if a game or music content designed for mobile phones holds one of the top five deck positions, it will certainly be mobbed. If WDA lets you turn the pike, then you must create publicity—in addition to the ads paid for by the carriers—in order to move your content into a top deck.

A handful of mobile games publishers are able to bypass WDA. Glu Mobile, Electronic Arts, IGN, Digital Chocolate, Hands On Mobile and Konami deal directly with the wireless carriers. They earned the right to bypass WDA by publishing consistently popular content.

The wireless carriers have their own regulations. These vary by carrier, and include prohibitions and fund-raising for charities such as the United Way as well as requiring that all subscription periods be monthly, not daily, weekly or annually. Verizon has the strictest censorship policy. It prohibits dating services as well as "unmoderated chatting, flirting and/or peer-to-peer communications services."

Once you get through the censors, the carriers will charge you a few pennies fee for every message you send your users, and charge them about 10 cents to receive your messages. Heavily visited online sites such as Craigslist.org could not have made it as a mobile community, but it could have worked for eBay, Amazon.com and thousands of online merchants. And perhaps they should begin parallel communities on the mobile networks as a defensive move against Verizon, Sprint Nextel, and AT&T treating their Internet properties just like their cell phone networks—charging fees and erecting barriers to entry, thus destroying a public good in the name of short-term profits. There are upstart wireless and Wi-Fi–based carriers such as Amp'd Mobile and Helio that could take market share from the established carriers. Helio is the brainchild of Sky Dayton, as sure an entrepreneur to wager on in wealth creation as Secretariat was at horse racing.

Off-Deck Marketing

If you read the 10-Qs and 10-Ks of the wireless carriers, you will see that content is steadily marching up the revenue graph and becoming a significant contributor to overall revenues. For Verizon, content now contributes approximately 16 percent of its revenues, up from 12.5 percent in early 2006.

Most of the wireless carriers have six or fewer people in their content departments. WDA does a lot of the heavy lifting for the carriers. Their business has traditionally been switching calls and earning pennies per minute. Content will be king pretty soon, and the wireless carriers will be more like Disney than AT&T. Peter Chernin, COO of News Corporation, upon News Corporation's acquisition of 51 percent of ringtone provider Jamba for $187.5 million in September 2006, said: "Mobile phones will become bigger carriers of media than television" (*Prepaid-Content*, September 20, 2006).

But there are smoke signals off in the distance from content developers that seek to market off-deck. They are developing games and prize-oriented social networks on their online communities, which you can port to your mobile phones with a credit card payment, thus obviating the need to visit the Lansing gatekeeper. Payment by e-wallet could get the wireless carriers' underwear in a knot. Sure, they will earn money from minutes, but will they lose on-deck control if off-deck marketing becomes popular? There is more chaos in the world of mobile communities and content shifting to wireless carriers and away from old media than in any giant market in the history of economics.

Bringing Back RSS

An old technology known as "really simple syndication," or RSS, is having a comeback, according to John Heilemann, a *Business 2.0* writer and keen observer of the "new" on the net. RSS is a very old push technology. It lets publishers stream Web content instantly to users who have subscribed to their feeds and lets users keep up with large numbers of sites without having to check them manually. When new content is posted on a site, subscribers are notified and sent either full versions or summaries of the fresh material, which they can read inside an aggregator such as NewsGator's FeedDemon. Both Firefox and Apple's Safari browser have built-in feed readers.

Dick Costolo is running with the notion of massive feeds and has launched FeedBurner, a personal content network, to enable "feeds of me" to the network. He says, "You put your tags in Del.icio.us, your photos in Flickr, your friends in AIM; you have a blog, a podcast, etc. And we splice it all together into a single feed" ("Branding the Feed," *Business 2.0*, July 2006, p. 44). His confidence can be summed up in what I will call Costolo's Law of Social Networks:

The new medium never drives dollars to the old; it drives dollars to the new thing.

Returning to rescuing Ford Motor Company, the secret sauce might be Costolo's Law. If Ford changed its dashboard to act more like a TV-set-top box, where drivers could demand individualized content, and if the new line of Ford vehicles looked sporty and made a new age statement (not "Ford Tough," for heaven's sake), might Ford become the auto manufacturer of the millennials? It could be that the automobile becomes the new and greatest carrier of media, trumping the mobile phone.

Will the Old Blow Their Money Buying the New?

Could old-media companies, such as News Corporation, be blowing their wad on expensive purchases of new communities? Will they find that users of their communities turn away from MySpace.com because it is no longer the newest thing? Will old media lose the trust that the community owners created when they were just barely meeting payroll?

The answer is that the network effect or buzz could kill their purchased communities if they overload the pages with old-media revenue-generating schemes. Too much advertising could kill the purchased communities. Too many relevant ads placed next to key phrases using a Google license could kill them. Media bragging and high salaries or perks paid to the executives who run the purchased communities could kill them.

Even new community owners must walk on eggs concerning capitalist events that occur to them. Bragging in the press about receiving millions of dollars of venture capital could be the death knell of a community that is being mobbed. Users of the community believe the community is "their" place, a place they share with people like themselves. Venture capitalists are not people like themselves but wealthy MBAs who, in some eyes, are avaricious vultures eager to force the community's founders to sell (or sell out) to old media, and when that occurs they will be bunched into demographic groups and pelted with old media's ads for sister TV shows and Google-licensed ads placed next to relevant phrases in profiles.

What the mob gives, the mob can take away. Some of the early social networks have lost much of their value because their backers and founders talked too much.

When the desire to toot your horn washes over you, lie down for 30 minutes repeating this mantra:

> *If I don't have to write it, I will speak it.*
> *If I don't have to speak it, I will whisper it.*
> *If I don't have to whisper it, I will nod.*

The media is in business to sell newspapers, not to glorify your accomplishments as a communiteer. As Lord Beaverbrook was quoted as saying when he launched the first tabloid on Fleet Street hundreds of years ago:

"It is the function of journalism to comfort the afflicted and bring affliction to the comfortable."

Summary

- Always appear poor; wear old clothes and shoes. Avoid haircuts.
- Generate an attack on your community from preachers, old media or the press in order to get the mob to come to you.
- New communities beckon new forms of revenue-generating: Why isn't the Gap accepting payment in synthetic money earned in online communities? Duh.
- New revenue-generating paradigms will be necessary because community users will demand it. These are:
  - Tip jar
  - Kudos
  - Reputation management fee
  - Syndication fees
  - Affinity credit cards
  - DRM fee
  - Users group charges
  - Revenue sharing
  - Strategic alliances
  - Facilities management
  - Port content to a wireless carrier.
- Mobile communities have the extra cash flow channel: wireless carriers that split the revenue they earn from your users 65/35 with you.
- Subscription fees are a possible source of revenues in restrictive communities, where there is a scarce resource to share.
- Selling ads on community pages is so yesterday. Community members want the new, not the old.

- The P2P platform will most likely become the network for many of the massively mobbed communities. You won't have to buy many servers.
- Struggling auto manufacturers should take a page from the playbooks of wireless carriers and become individualized content carriers. In WiMAXed communities such as Tempe, Arizona, broadband is ubiquitous.
- Communiteers must remember to always appear poor, but continue to disrupt established industries in order to tie their underwear into knots.

Rules for Creating
Successful Business Models

Trust is the only capital you have to spend when you launch your community.

—David Silver

AT THIS POINT, you may be thinking about the community you would like to launch. But before leaping into the great unknown, take the test that I have created in this chapter. The scoring system enables an entrepreneur to determine in advance if a new community is worth the time, effort and capital to launch, or if it should be shelved.

As you use the following questions to analyze the new community that you are planning to launch, hold up its key components to the mirror that my scoring system presents. A perfect score of 45 means an extremely high probability of success, with very little reliance on angel capital, and a valuation in three years approaching $500 million, and in five years exceeding $1 billion. Several old, off-line communities as well as the amazing eBay are perfect 45s: Arthur Murray Dance Studios, Rotary Clubs International, Weight Watchers International, Tupperware, Dow Jones, the New York Stock Exchange, NASDAQ and Mary Kay

Cosmetics come immediately to mind. If your business model scores 35 or more, I recommend that you launch it. And you had best move with alacrity, because really big ideas don't just sit there without someone capitalizing on them.

The First Law of Entrepreneurship

The first and most critical test is Silver's First Law of Entrepreneurship, which says that valuation (V), or wealth if you prefer, is equal to the size of the problem (P) that you have identified, times the elegance of the solution (S) that will be sold to those who have the problem, times the judgment of the entrepreneurial team (E):

$$V = P \times S \times E$$

Because these three factors are multiplied rather than added, a zero or negative value for either P, S, or E wipes out the company from the beginning. If you think of the hundreds of dot-com wipeouts retrospectively, all were missing positive values for P, S or E or sometimes all three.

P, S and E have four possible values: 3 is the highest, 2 is the mid-level, 1 is low; and zero is the absence of value, to wit:

Size of the Problem

3 = large—multiply the number of people with the problem times the price they would pay for a solution ($1 billion or more is large)

2 = medium ($250 m to $900 m)

1 = small (under $250m)

Elegance of the Solution

3 = nonduplicable, first to market, difficult to replicate

2 = first to market, difficult to replicate

1 = first to market

Experience of the Entrepreneurial Team

3 = entrepreneurial team has managed a launch before, knows how to operate a company

2 = entrepreneurial team has at least one person who has launched and operated a company before

1 = entrepreneurial team has no prior launch experience

If the new company scores $3 \times 3 \times 3$, it is off to the best start possible. An entrepreneurial team that scores a 3 is likely to direct itself to a problem that also scores a 3. It has a high probability of success addressing a problem with a score of 2, but it will likely grow bored and break up if it attempts to solve a problem that scores only a 1. A solution that scores a 3 has the three most important factors of any new business going for it: defense against possible competitors, uniqueness or nonreplicability, and a head start in the race. Even if the size of the problem or the experience of the entrepreneurial team doesn't score a 3, a solution that scores a 3, which means it is proprietary and protected, can always be sold to a buyer, whether it ever achieves the stage of commercial success or not.

The Size of the Problem

There are many problems in search of entrepreneurial-driven solutions; in fact, that is where most solutions to society's problems come from— the insight, energy, judgment and drive of entrepreneurs. But problems that can be solved by aggregating people into an online or mobile community are a whole 'nother kettle of fish.

If everything we need to know to solve life's many problems already exists and does not have to be invented, discovered or built but is out there somewhere, then by aggregating people into crowds and accepting the hypothesis that there is great wisdom in crowds, solutions should eventually be found to every problem. Although this hypothesis cannot possibly be true because it would assume the finiteness of problems, even if it is partially true, say one-tenth true, then there are many communities that can be launched to bring people together to rub up against each other, create molecular energy, let sparks fly and arrive at some elegant solutions.

For a while, online and mobile communities will be fun-oriented, and that is to be expected. Every society since the beginning of time has had its music, its games and its art. To these will be added hunter-gatherer activities, food preparation, spiritual events, medical research, and the sharing of wealth-protection information and gossip or reputation management in all its various forms. Follow the evolution of humankind, read *Foucalt's Pendulum*, study the guilds and associations of the fifteenth through the nineteenth centuries, and you will see how problems were addressed through collaborative efforts pre-Internet and cellular phone. Copy one or two of these models, and fasten your seat belt for takeoff.

In measuring the size of the problem that you will attempt to solve, first determine the number of people who suffer from the problem, and assume they would pay $20 per year to alleviate it or eliminate it from their lives. If 20 million people suffer from the problem, then the size of the opportunity that you are addressing is:

$$20,000,000 \times \$20 = \$400,000,000$$

If you can add several more revenue channels to the $20 per annum subscription fee, then you are addressing an opportunity in the billion-dollar range. You will definitely want to move swiftly to capture the lion's share of this huge market.

It is often the case in conceiving entrepreneurial opportunities that your solution can address two needs. For example, I am a fan of the University of Tennessee Volunteers football team. However, I live in northern New Mexico and cannot get a daily dose of Knoxville sports radio talk shows to satiate my need for Southeastern Conference sports gossip, injury reports and the like. I would pay $20 a *month* to access a content player on the dashboard of my car for 30 minutes a day and then listen to a play-by-play of the game on Saturday. I would visit the community that offered me this, plus "Rocky Top," the Volunteers' fight song, as my ringtone. I am certain that I'm not the only fan of Division 1 sports who lives thousands of miles from the university that he loves; there have got to be hundreds of thousands of old failed jocks like me yearning for the sounds and smells of old Ivy on an autumn Saturday afternoon. Now, that's a scarce resource many people would pay for.

The entrepreneur who brings this solution to me will need to license the content from the universities—not a terribly difficult assignment, since it is "found money" to them. He will have to line up some advertisers to supplement the subscription fees that I and the other old failed jocks pay. And then he will have to convince the people like me to pay a subscription up front, to reduce the need for capital. That's a three-part sale: License the content from 250 university athletic departments, find sponsors who want to reach this particular market of old failed jocks, and collect money from the users. Once the old failed jocks are happily involved in the gossip, jibes, predictions, coaches' interviews, injury reports and nuances of the season, they will generate a lot of content from their glory days on campus and perhaps begin trading memorabilia. New marketing opportunities could open up, enlarging revenues still further.

Always be open for multilinear, multichannel entrepreneurial opportunities. They are complex to pull off, and it is often that level of complexity that serves as your buffer and keeps competitors from entering the marketplace against you.

The Elegance of the Solution

It is not only complexity that keeps competitors at bay—it is more often *dumbness*. For example, when Fred Smith launched FedEx, his solution involved flying all packages to a central hub in Memphis, Tennessee, then sorting them at the hub, and putting them on new planes in the early morning hours to be flown to the intended destinations.

Young Fred was laughed at by the senior managers of Emery Air Freight and Purolator Express. They called his business model "dumb." They did not emulate FedEx because they thought the business model would fail for being too dumb, simplistic, foolish and not worthy of copying. Emery Air Freight and Purolator Express have gone out of business while FedEx has achieved the status of being eponymous for "Send it quickly and with certainty."

Nobody in the personal health and fitness field copied Jean Nidetch when she started Weight Watchers International on the premise that overweight people would willingly pay her two dollars to drive downtown to a hotel conference room and stand up in a room full of overweight people to complain about how fat they had become. In less than five years, Mrs. Nidetch's company and brand had a recognition factor of 91 percent. Her solution was delivered very elegantly, and she did not brag about it to the media. She kept a very low profile.

The same quiet beauty appears in the extraordinarily elegant Arthur Murray Dance Studios business. The users provide the outfits, music, dancing shoes, and travel costs, and they expend the energy to dance. The Arthur Murray franchisee rents an empty room, turns on the lights, brings the music player and some of the music, and collects the fees from the dancers. How beautiful a business is that? And the model can be replicated online and in mobile social networks. Sonic Branding Solutions does it.

A vital component of delivering an elegant solution is to do it quietly and without publicity. If you raise capital, do not advertise it. If you capture a million users, keep your mouth shut. Be silent and remain so until you are much larger. Subscribers to online and mobile communities will give you their trust and some form of payment if you appear small, like a rookie, somewhat naïve, and iconoclastic toward installed old media, rather than a suck-up to old media. They will help you build your community through trust and word-of-mouth marketing, but you must reward their trust at the most trenchantly gut level—by earning it and never selling them out with old-media tactics such as carpet bombing them with ads or renting their names to e-spammers.

The Judgment of Entrepreneurs

The greatest thinker and writer on the subject of management, Peter H. Drucker, wrote: "Managers must know how to do the right thing. They can hire people to do things right."

When you launch your online or mobile community, you will become a manager perhaps for the first time. The most important actions you will take each day—and there will be 25 or more decisions to make each day—will require you to do the right thing. You will often have to make these decisions on the fly or while multitasking. That is very difficult, and my best advice to you is to put off the decisions until your head is clear and your phones aren't ringing off their hooks. If you need to call on the advice of a mentor or trusted friend before acting, then do so. Your judgment will get better over time and you will be able to make decisions more quickly.

Putting together an entrepreneurial team is critical. You will need allies "to do things right" such as a chief technology officer (CTO) and a bookkeeper or CFO, and perhaps a head of sales and marketing or of content licensing or someone to work with the wireless carriers. The stronger the skill sets of your first two or three hires, the more successful your company will become.

At the risk of being repetitive, the purpose of being in business, rather than being a poet or Andean trekker, is *to make your product or service a substitute for all other competitive products or services and to make their products or services no substitute for yours.*

Change "your" and "yours" to "our" and "ours," type the phrase in boldface print, and paste it up on the water cooler in your new office. For there is no other reason to go to work every day than this.

The Eight DEJ Factors

Briefly, *DEJ* stands for demonstrable economic justification, and there are eight factors that make up this test. If your new company has fewer than six of these DEJ factors, it will require tens and perhaps hundreds of millions of dollars, and its probability of succeeding is less than 60 percent, and descending as the number of DEJ factors descends.

The eight DEJ factors are as follows, with very short explanations:

1. *Existence of a large number of receivers.* Are there many potential consumers of your solution, and are they aware of the problem that your solution addresses?
2. *Homogeneity of receivers.* Will the consumers of your solution accept a standard product or service, or will you have to customize it?

3. *Existence of qualified receivers.* If you select a market in which the receivers don't know they have a problem, you will need megabucks to educate them. You want buyers who do not have to be told they have a problem; they know they have a problem, and know they have to pay for a solution.

4. *Existence of competent providers.* Will the solution delivery system require expensive salespeople and a long cycle from presentation to sale, or can merely competent salespersons make the sale quickly?

5. *Absence of institutional barriers to entry.* Is there a restriction that must be removed before the product or service can be introduced to the market? An example would be the United States Food and Drug Administration, which must approve all new drugs and medical devices prior to their sale in the United States.

6. *The "Hey, it really works!" factor.* Will marketing the product or service require advertising on a grand scale, or will the benefits of the product or service get passed along by word of mouth?

7. *Invisibility.* Can the new company be built stone by stone quietly, or will news leak out to possible competitors accidentally or intentionally, the latter because of the company being publicly held or the subject of publicity and conversations with the press?

8. *Optimum price/cost factor.* Does the product or service have a relatively high gross profit margin—above 80 percent, for instance—so that there will be considerable cash flow to deploy toward marketing?

The scoring system is the function of multiplying the values of the three factors in Silver's First Law of Entrepreneurship and adding the quotient thus derived to the sum of the DEJ Factors. For instance, if the quotient is $3 \times 2 \times 2$, or 12, and your new company has seven of the eight DEJ Factors, your Silver score so far is $12 + 7$ or 19, a moderately high score.

Using Boosters

You can boost your community's probability of success by deploying the strategies of "Float Many Clubs." Moreover, you can minimize the amount of capital needed by increasing the amount of float you raise from customers and vendors. *Float* can achieve a value of 6, *Many* is worth 2 points and *Clubs* is worth 2 points in this scoring system.

Float is one of the entrepreneurs' favorite words. It means using the customers' payments for a while before delivering the product or service. Some of the solution delivery methods that are based on customer financing include subscription selling, franchising, membership clubs, facilities management and party-plan selling (this is sometimes referred to as multilevel marketing). Most businesses launched by women rely on float, because women have not been favored with venture capital, and thus have ineluctably asked their customers to pay up front. Vendors who are willing to wait 120 days to be paid also provide float.

Once you study the many methods of using float and expanding the sources of float—and there are many—your new company will be able to minimize its reliance on venture capital and increase its probability of success. Ray Kroc, builder of McDonald's, was the master of float, which he codified as franchising and obviated his need for venture capital. In creating an online community you must establish up front that the community provides valuable benefits to its members. Many communities that provide important benefits to their members will be launched with the sale of annual subscriptions for $1.66 per month or $20 per year. You will be able to do many good things for your members if they provide you with $20 per year.

Generating Float

Float is cash paid to your community from members in advance of their receiving your product or service. Thousands of ISPs were launched on float in the form of subscription fees charged before the monthly service was provided. According to some ISP owners, they ordered a server from Sun or Cobalt with every 50 checks of $20—one month's subscription fee—in anticipation of the next 50 sign-ups. If the ISPs required more cash, they offered their subscribers the opportunity to purchase an annual subscription for $200. With many ISPs now expanding into broadband wireless, and converting $14 a month dial-up subscribers to $40 a

month broadband subscribers, and Motorola Canopy receivers and trans-
mitter sets requiring $500 a pop, the ISPs are scrambling for float once
again. If they have clean financial statements, local banks or equipment
leasing companies will provide them with float, in the form of equipment
loans or leases.

Mobile-based communities are paid for by their subscribers, but the
payments are typically collected by the wireless carriers and paid to the
communities after the service is delivered, sometimes 90 days later. Local
banks and commercial finance companies are just beginning to see the
opportunity and are loaning money to mobile-based community companies. San Jose–based Bridge Bank has spotted this opportunity to make
loans (provide float) to mobile communities. "We like these borrowers,"
Scott Chamberlin, Bridge's vice president, told me as a portfolio company CEO and I sat in his office borrowing money for a mobile social
network a few months ago.

Online communities often begin by aggregating lots of members but
do not have a revenue model that provides them with float. Venture capitalists have seen this situation as an opportunity for them to provide
growth capital. Doing so bends a hallowed rule of venture capital investing: Invest only in companies with a proven and sustainable revenue
model with a high gross profit margin.

Yet with a mere $3 million in revenues from ads, 18-month-old
digg.com, a gatherer of news for members to use to aggregate their favorite stories, raised venture capital at a valuation of $200 million. Mark
Zuckerberg, the founder of Facebook.com, a social network for the college crowd, raised $25 million in venture capital at a valuation of $500
million, without a proven and sustainable business model. YouTube.com
raised $11.5 million in venture capital without a proven and sustainable
business model from a syndicate led by Sequoia Capital, arguably the
most successful venture capital fund on the planet.

There are many other ways for online communities to generate float,
without having to raise venture capital. One is to provide the names
(pseudonyms) and the mobile phone numbers (they will have to ask for
these) to mobile-based communities with content that will be of interest

to the members of the online communities. For MySpace.com and Face-book.com members, the content could be:

- Location and facts concerning parties in their cities.
- Location and facts concerning concerts in their cities.
- Indie music that is being heavily downloaded.
- "Mobbed" indie videos.
- Prizes for the first 100 members who enter a contest and score high points.

The online community could ask the mobile community to pay up front for the cost of slicing and dicing its names and uploading them to the mobile community. It will have to be determined in advance if the online community is paid a finders fee when its members sign up to become members of the mobile community.

Then the really good news is that the wireless carriers will earn minutes from new mobile phone users—those at MySpace.com and Facebook.com—when they enjoy the content offered by the mobile community. The more minutes they stay connected, and share the information about the massive party and the new Indie musician who really rocks, the more revenues the mobile community collects and pays to the online community.

Let's take an example. Assume that MySpace.com rents one-tenth of its members—for example, 7 million people whose profiles indicate they live in the New York, northern New Jersey, southern Connecticut market, and they love dancing—to Sonic Branding Solutions, a provider of music games and ringtone dance parties, including many in the New York metropolitan area. Then, if 7 million, or 10 percent, of MySpace.com names spend two hours a month for three months connected to an event at Sonic Branding Solutions, and sharing with their friends, creating a new ringtone and going to a ringtone dance party once a week, the revenues generated by this partnership will be roughly $14 million for the 90-day period, of which MySpace.com and Sonic Branding Solutions will each receive $3.5 million for the trial period and four times that for the year if they agree to extend the partnership. My-Space provides an unexpected reward to its members, thus increasing their loyalty; and it adds a new revenue channel.

Cutting deals like this provides float to the collaborating communities. It's not rocket science; it's just a new spin on the list rental business, where magazine publishers obtain lots of names from Publishers Clearing House and other mass marketers and collectors of tens of millions of names.

At the risk of being repetitive, remember not to discuss relationships such as this, or any contracts with any source of capital or money or names, with the media or anyone outside your company, because the story could come out negatively to the detriment of all parties.

Many Revenue Channels

In the "Float Many Clubs" formula, *many* means that there are numerous channels through which to generate revenues for your new company's service, but you have to explore these opportunities and then grab the ones that provide cash up front. There are certain kinds of solution delivery methods—or *business models*, if you prefer the simpler phrase—that expand the market with each sale your company makes, and there are others that shrink the market with each sale your company makes. Most new companies are launched with the shrink-the-market business model. But they can be converted to the expand-the-market model from the outset by opening 5, 10 or 20 additional channels up front. In other words, if you capture a new member, you have shrunk the universe of potential customers by one. But if you gain multiple revenue channels by having added the one new member, you have expanded your market by one.

Licensing large, related companies to market your company's product or service in foreign or selected vertical markets is one way of achieving this. Launching a users group and having customers join the users group and pay a users group fee is another means. There are dozens of strategies for opening new cash flow channels, and with each one that you open you increase your probability of success and reduce your reliance on venture capital.

Bring the Members Together

Club refers to ways to enhance membership and raise the prospect of reward by lowering the risk. Newsletters are one way of doing this. Many entrepreneurs miss the opportunity to ask their customers to subscribe to a monthly newsletter that catalogues the events of the month, provides the names of turnstile jumpers and provides a suggestion box in which members suggest means of improving the community. Once the newsletter becomes something that the members look forward to, it can be expanded into a magazine, with ads, and from there into a trade show. Now you're talking big dollars. Trade shows are living magazines.

The combination of magazines and trade shows can generate up to 24 additional cash flow channels for the new company including subscriptions, advertisements, classifieds, endorsement fees, sponsorship fees and many more. For the entrepreneur who adds newsletters and/or magazines to his business model, multiple revenue channels bring in cash every day and night of the week, while the employees are sleeping, much of it at very high gross profit margins, thus enhancing the company's probability of success while minimizing its reliance on capital.

Once you understand the principles of "Float Many Clubs" you can roll out a fuller, fatter business model with much higher aggregate revenue and cash flow projections and you can move a Silver score in the 25 to 30 range, which is moderate, to a 35 to 40 range, which is high. The highest possible Silver score is, of course, $3 \times 3 \times 3 = 27 + 8 + 10 = 45$. We would all like to begin with 45, but that happy event is extremely rare. A community whose business model achieves a score of 45 has no need to raise venture capital, while achieving a valuation of more than $1 billion in less than 10 years.

Formulating the Problem

"Ready, fire, aim" is a big mistake in launching a new company. Stay in the "Ready, ready, ready" stage for a while. The other term for "Ready, ready, ready" is *problem formulation*. Entrepreneurship is not creating a solution to a problem already defined. Rather, it is the formulation and reformulation of the problem until a solution emerges through the process of raising all of the questions, examining the problem from all angles, and restating and reframing the problem until it has been examined as thoroughly as possible. The entrepreneur who formulates the problem in a thorough, exhaustive manner will develop a larger P factor—that is, the size of the problem (P) or opportunity will grow larger—and the S factor, the solutions, will become more elegant than will those of the entrepreneur who invents a superior S without examining all of the nooks and crannies of P.

If the process of entrepreneurial creativity is to be understood fully, the study of what the entrepreneur does cannot be restricted to the visible solution, the finished product. It must include the earlier, crucial step: formulation of the problem to which the solution is a response. In addition, the formulation of the problem is not a constant but, rather, a cumulative process of discovery that begins when the potential entrepreneur enters the period of dissatisfaction at what she is currently doing to earn a living, extends through the development of insight into the problem, and often does not end until the entrepreneurial company she has built is a smoothly running, well-oiled machine.

Thinking, we know, is equated with rational, methodical, unadventurous problem solving; the unfolding of symbolic links from given premises to known conclusions. Creative thinking does not follow the known path. Rather than accepting the premises of a structured problem, creativity fashions a new problematic configuration. Instead of striving to reach a known solution, the cognitive efforts of a creative person are frequently targeted at goals that previously had been considered inconceivable or not achievable. If behavioral scientists skilled in structuring measurement systems would observe entrepreneurs at work, query them continually, and qualify and correlate the results against standards, we would learn more about the creative process that entrepreneurship involves than we would from my or any other lay observations.

One method of measurement would be to put 20 significant problems on pieces of paper, have the entrepreneurs select the one that they would like to build a business to solve, and then formulate the business plan. The launch itself would require capital aplenty, not a long commodity at universities these days; thus, measuring the competence of an entrepreneur by the success of the business against his or her creative process will probably have to be postponed until there is funding for the full study. Still, behavioral science is sufficiently developed to measure the creativity of the entrepreneurial process.

Hiring Corporate Achievers to Run the Company

You must hire the best and most experienced managers you can find to run your enterprise. A unifying factor is that all members of the team want to build a successful company. The manager's goals are perhaps more positive cash flow oriented, while the entrepreneur's goal is to do some one thing extremely well. But the partners need each other for several very important reasons, not the least of which are (1) entrepreneurs need managers around to direct their talents, focus their energies, and orchestrate the increasing number of people and departments; and (2) managers need energetic, innovative, imaginative entrepreneurs to provide them with growing companies to which they can apply their managerial talents.

The entrepreneurial team works somewhat as follows: Two people decide to go on a photographic safari in Africa. The first person boards the plane in casual attire, unburdened by carry-on luggage. The second carries six cameras, two filters, 20 guidebooks, camping equipment, a tent and other paraphernalia. The plane lands in Kenya and the two set off on foot into the jungle. The first traveler goes out in front and the second decides to stop and put up the tent. The first is about a mile away from where the tent is being set up when a tiger jumps out from behind a tree, growls, and charges. The first traveler spins around and runs back to the tent as fast as he can, with the tiger in hot pursuit. The tent is partway up, and the tiger's would-be prey runs into the tent, swings around the pole, and heads out in the same direction, shouting back at the detail-oriented partner: "This tiger is for you. I'm going to go back for mine."

Entrepreneurs can generate weeks of work in the first three hours of the day, drop it off on the manager's desk to be organized and implemented, and then change their minds by the afternoon. Wise managers are delighted for the opportunity to clean up after the entrepreneurs. They are used to making management decisions; now, for the first time, they own a meaningful portion of the company that they manage.

This pattern of the fast-thinking, fast-moving, quick-to-judge entrepreneur and the patient, thorough, careful corporate achiever manager is replicated time and again in the world of early-stage companies. It has the benefit of two forces counterbalancing one another and wrestling with the options of choosing this's and that's. Give some serious thought to this management model when starting your community. It could mean the difference between success and failure. Eric Schmidt's seasoned perspective added immense value to the inventive Page-Brin team that founded Google.

Raising Capital

Strategic Partnering

As one of the major themes of this book is cooperation, I will take you through the keys of successful strategic partnering, which is the use of cooperation as the primary revenue generator and capital provider in your business model. Large consumer products marketing companies will be falling all over themselves to form alliances with entrepreneurial companies that are forming communities of consumers that the large corporations would give their eyeteeth to place products in front of. Many new communities will be launched on behalf of automobile manufacturers, consumer products marketers and consumer service companies (i.e., Fortune 500 companies, exclusive of industrial manufacturers). They need community members, and they will be aggressively looking for you.

The importance of strategic partnering cannot be overstressed. This method of raising capital is essentially licensing with hormones. In classical product or service licensing, the entrepreneurial company develops a proprietary way of solving a problem, then licenses its solution to existing companies in the industry to make, use and sell its product or service, and collects royalties over time. The large company, known as the licensee, sells the innovative solution through its established marketing

"On the Internet, nobody knows you're a dog."

channels in a proscribed geographic region or in predetermined vertical markets.

If that were all there was to it, these alliances would be nothing more than licensing agreements (yawn). But the entrepreneurial companies are demanding—and getting—corporate venture capital investments concomitant with signing the licensing agreements. Moreover, the venture capital investments are being made at eye-popping valuations—on the order of $10 million for ownership of 10 percent, or less, of the entrepreneurial company's common stock.

From the large corporation's point of view, the reasons and requirements for the investment along with the agreement to make, use and sell the young company's product are as follows:

- We want you to be financially sound so that you can focus on new product development and upgrades.
- We appreciate that you are able to innovate new and useful products, and bring them to market more efficiently, less expensively, and faster than we can by an order of magnitude.
- We want to be kept informed, just as any stockholder is entitled to, about your financial health, budgets, plans—and if any of your competitors have gotten their noses under your tent.
- We do not want you talking to any of our competitors about your innovative products or your plans. We want your complete attentiveness.
- We may want to acquire you some day, and by paying a little bit for some of your stock today, we could lower our overall acquisition price later on.

The corporate venture capital investment is separate and apart from *payments* made by the large corporation to the entrepreneurial company under the terms of the licensing agreement. Note the emphasis on the word *payments*. If you are receiving only one form of payment from the licensee, you are leaving some money on the table.

From the point of view of the entrepreneurial company, some key elements to include in the licensing agreement are the following:

- Proscribe the geographic market or vertical industry in which the licensee can sell the product.
- Clarify whether the license is to make, use, and sell, or just to sell (with the entrepreneurial company keeping the right to make the product and sell it to the licensee). Try to hold on to the right to produce, and to sell the product to the licensee for an additional cash flow channel.

- Set a precise time period for the term of the license, such as five years.
- Set exact minimum annual royalties. This is a difficult number to negotiate but it is your means of breaking the agreement if the licensee you selected is incapable of selling the product. The licensee could grow tired of paying the minimum annual royalties, while you may wish to release it from the contract and find a better partner.
- Demand and receive a right to audit the licensee's books and records to make sure the royalties paid to you are accurate. The cost of the audit should be the licensee's if the dollar amount you have been shorted is large, say over $20,000. Otherwise, it should be the licensor's cost.
- You demand an up-front payment equal to one-half of the licensee's estimated first-year royalty payments to the entrepreneurial company. The logic for this is that it is awfully expensive to audit the licensee. So, to avoid disputes at the back end, you need a show of good faith up front.
- Set precise minimum sales targets on which royalties are based, and have the licensee agree to pay the entrepreneurial company the minimum each year (or half-year or quarter-year), whether the licensee actually makes the sales or not.
- Clearly delineate events of default. Set these out in writing, and take back the license if the licensee defaults.
- As consideration, the entrepreneurial company may have to give a right of first refusal to the licensee on any and all new or related products, share related R&D data, and agree to other restrictions on freedom of movement. You may be able to charge for some of these add-ons, especially if they restrict your freedom to deal with others.

If large corporations could innovate with speed and efficiency, and pinpoint their markets' needs, as well as entrepreneurial companies, there would be no need for their entering into strategic alliances. But they cannot bring new products to market as well as entrepreneurial companies can. By the same token, entrepreneurial companies need marketing channels, knowledge of the market, multiple sales offices, production capabilities, foreign markets, laboratories, warehouse space, and capital. Large corporations have all these facilities.

The Reasons for Strategic Partnering

Whereas venture capital funds invest for the purpose of achieving significantly higher than conventional returns for taking significantly greater than typical investment risks, strategic partners invest in entrepreneurial companies for the following reasons:

- To incubate and reduce the cost of acquisitions.
- To gain exposure to possible new markets.
- To add new products to existing distribution channels.
- To reduce the cost of research and development through strategic partnering.
- To expose middle management to entrepreneurship.
- To obtain a management training area for bright young trainees in need of experience.
- To utilize excess manufacturing capacity, space, or computer time.
- To mesh the activities of several departments in joint efforts.
- To generate capital gains.
- To "look through the window of innovation"—to develop antennae for breakthrough technologies.
- To generate income through strategic partnering (if it is competently managed).
- To provide excellent group therapy for senior management.
- To create good public relations by reflecting forward-looking management.
- To keep pace with their competition, who are probably doing it.
- The ITEK reason. (Several employees of Eastman Kodak developed a breakthrough product and showed it to senior management, who disapproved of it and told the employees they were wasting their time. So the employees left, named their new company "ITEK" for "I Took Eastman Kodak" and made hundreds of millions of dollars.)
- To encourage new company formation in the community.

These reasons, given to me by corporate officials, are not all-inclusive, but they are the ones most often cited in descending order by the most active corporate strategic partners.

More Capital: Less Give-Up

Strategic investors generally seek meaningfully smaller ownership positions in entrepreneurial companies than do financial investors. This situation exists because strategic investors become involved in entrepreneurial companies for reasons other than pure capital gain, while financial investors are interested solely and completely in capital gain. The axiom "Strategic investors always pay more than financial investors" is true. Believe it. But strategic investors get more bang for their buck if they *cooperate* with the entrepreneurial company.

Raising Capital from Angel Investors

Angel investors are wealthy individuals, many of them former entrepreneurs, who love the *chase*. Sure, they want to make a terrific return on their investment, but they want to advise the entrepreneurs, whom they back with capital, push up toll gates at hard-to-contact institutions and corporations, and use their golden Rolodexes to introduce the entrepreneurs to important contacts. By being useful to the companies that they invest in, the angels stay in the game, participate in the chase and cooperate with their co-investors in conference calls with the entrepreneurial management team.

Some of the angel investors in the Santa Fe Capital Group club tell me that they're not in it for the money, of which they have quite a bit. They're in it to be able to tell their buddies at the 19th hole, "Yeah, I'm in a VoIP deal that's kicking Telco's butt, and I've got some money in a social networking deal." It makes them feel young and vital as well as one up on their golfing buddies.

I have managed a group of angel investors named Santa Fe Capital Group for more than 20 years and we have had a wonderful time working with entrepreneurs all over the world, fueling their dream machines.

Many of the insights I have learned in my angel investing work have come from the entrepreneurs that our group has backed.

There are five stages in the growth of an entrepreneurial company. Angel investors generally invest at stage two, after the new product or service has been conceived. See Figure 7.1.

Angel Investors Attempt to Avert Risk

There are typically five risks in a start-up or early-stage company that correspond to the five stages of development depicted in Figure 7.1. Angel investors typically accept risks 2 through 4. It is up to the venture capitalist to accept no more than the last three of these risks, and the two

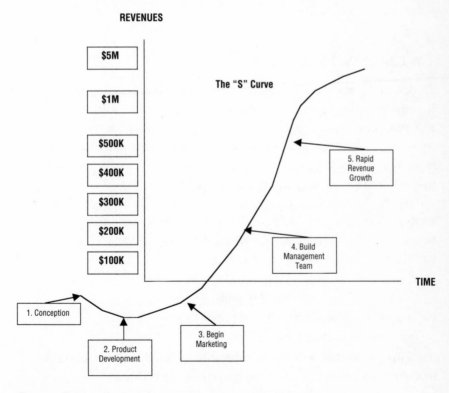

FIGURE 7.1   The Five Stages of an Entrepreneurial Company

that the venture capitalist can control most effectively are the third and fourth: marketing and management. The five risks are:

1. The conception risk: Can we develop the product?
2. The development risk: If we can develop it, can we produce it?
3. The marketing risk: If we can make it, can we sell it?
4. The management risk: If we can sell it, can we sell it at a profit?
5. The growth risk: If we can manage the company, can we grow it?

The acceptable risks are marketing, management and growth because they are the most controllable. The conception risk is borne by the entrepreneurs and funded with their savings and family's and friends' capital. Angel investors accept four risks, and mitigate these risks by providing advice and guidance.

The Law of the Hockey Stick

To determine the amount of ownership that the angel investor requires in order to make a given investment, which is another way of measuring valuation, many angel investors rely on the hockey stick method. It derives its name from the observation that all financial statement projections look like hockey sticks. The present undercapitalized company is at the toe and the rosy future is up at the handle.

Figure 7.2 is a descriptive drawing that amplifies the hockey stick method of pricing early-stage investment opportunities. In this diagram, the need for capital is $1.5 million and the third-year projected net profit after taxes is $2 million. The formula is:

$$\frac{\text{Amount of angel capital} \times 5}{\text{Third-year net profit after taxes} \times 10 \text{ or } 12}$$

This equals the percentage ownership required by the angel investor to meet a conventional return on investment (ROI) goal.

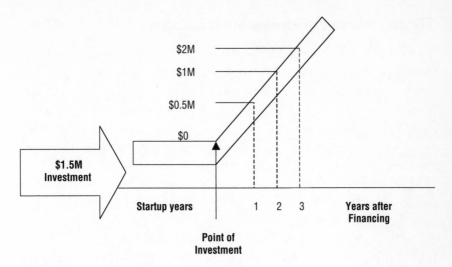

$2M

$1M

$0.5M

$0

$1.5M
Investment

Startup years   1   2   3   Years after
                                          Financing

Point of
Investment

FIGURE 7.2   Hockey Stick Method of Pricing the Deal

In Figure 7.2, use the earnings multiple of 10 to 12 to get equity give-up of 35 percent of company ownership. This multiple range is relatively low, but remember I am an angel investor. An entrepreneur would always select a higher earnings multiple in order to reduce the amount of equity ownership he is willing to give up for the investment. It's a tug-of-war, and the tougher the entrepreneur negotiates, the more the angel investor falls in love with the deal. Guts are respected.

If you want to reference-check what I am like to deal with as an angel investor, do not ask my competitors. I was fortunate to have the late Milton Friedman as a professor in business school at the University of Chicago. I'll remind you of one of Dr. Friedman's brilliant rules: "You can always pick out a professional from a pack of people. He is the one who, when he must compliment another member of his profession, such as a fellow economist, will usually heap effusive praise on all of his skills and hobbies, except the very one that he practices professionally." So it goes in the angel capital profession. Friendly competition prevents our heaping praise on another of our persuasion.

Thomas Watson's Curious Miscalculation

There really are no eureka moments in the entrepreneur business. Google provides an online advertising service, but it did not begin that way in the minds of Sergey Brin and Larry Page, its founders. Thomas Watson, the founder of IBM, thought IBM might sell five computers. Fred Smith, the founder of FedEx, thought that delivering blood from blood banks to hospitals was going to be a major revenue channel. Entrepreneurship is more of a pinball game than it appears to be.

Entrepreneurs, it has been said, are like the U.S. Marines landing on Iwo Jima in World War II. They fire in all directions, and if something falls, they run in that direction.

Spend a lot of time on problem formulation. Change your assumptions continually. Move the chess pieces around. Remember that you are a colonist in the second age of the Internet—the age of creating sustainable colonies in a new world.

Follow the *artists* because they always lead cultural change.

Form a community in which the users believe it is their space, and they will automatically *cooperate* with one another, if there is a *reputation manager* to maintain the standards of the community.

Do not up-sell your customers to buy ancillary products, until you initially build a *primitive* colony in which they feel comfortable.

And, finally, you are a *colonist* and you are aggregating other colonists to join with you. The community is new to you and new to your customers. You are their Diogenes. Listen to their feedback. Find their needs. Service their needs.

A Venture Capital Return

A *venture capital return* is a compound rate of return of 30 percent per annum. This translates into three times the investor's initial investment returned to him in five years. For example, if the investor invests $1 million in January 2007, he seeks $4 million back in January 2010—the money plus $3 million. The relationship of compound annual rate of return, or yield on investment, to "times return," is demonstrated in Figure 7.3.

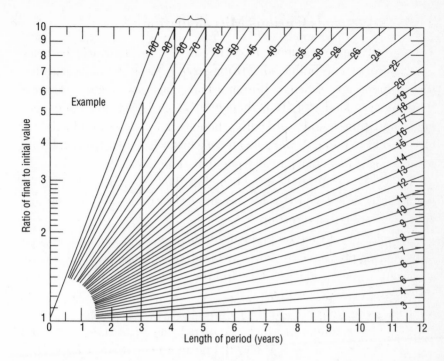

FIGURE 7.3   Target Rates of Return of a Typical Venture Capital Fund

The 30 percent compound annual rate of return target could translate into a hefty equity give-up to the entrepreneur. As an example, pretend you are starting a new company (we'll call it Newco) and that you have calculated a need for $1.5 million in venture capital. You prepare a business plan that describes the problem your company intends to solve, the solution that you have conceived, and the management team that you have assembled to carry out the plan. Your operating statement projections suggest that your company might earn $1 million after taxes in the fifth year, as shown in Table 7.1.

With $1 million in after-tax earnings in the fifth year, the venture capitalist investigates the possible exit strategies for the investment. These usually consist of the acquisition of the company by a larger, usually publicly-held company; taking the company public; or selling the in-

TABLE 7.1   Newco's Projected
Earnings in Its First Years of
Operation

Year	Net Profit (Loss) after Taxes ($ Thousands)
Year 1	−1,000
Year 2	−200
Year 3	275
Year 4	835
Year 5	1,000

vestment back to the company. The exit strategy most preferred is acquisition because it pays out cash or salable common stock to you and to the
venture capital investor.

The second most preferable option is to take the company public.
Most underwriters of initial public offerings will not permit insiders to
sell their stock at the first offering; the investment cannot be converted
into cash, but into "near cash." You and your backers, as insiders, are limited as such by Rule 144 of the Securities and Exchange Commission to
dribbling out a small fraction of your ownership until a one-year time period passes. But if the price paid for your company's common stock is
more than the price paid by the venture capitalists, they can mark up the
value of the investment on their books, which means a higher management fee for the partners of the fund. Their fees—salaries and money to
operate with—are generally 3.5 percent of the net asset value of their
fund. Venture capitalists love marking up the value of their investments;
it's the next best thing to selling their stock for cash.

Summary

As an alternative to float and an additional source of up-front cash, visit
with a company in the industry your community will disrupt, and offer
to assist them in entering the community business. This strategic alliance provides them with many good things and they should be willing

to invest $1 million in your community's common stock as consideration for receiving the benefits.

Then, if you need angel capital to build out your community, follow the hockey stick model, which has been a tried-and-true valuation method for 50 years.

In the next chapter, I describe a scenario in which a community that is popular among teenage girls can help an old-line corporation in the cosmetics industry launch a radically successful online and mobile community. The example speaks volumes about the triumph of cooperation over competition.

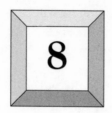

How to Launch a New Product

THERE ARE A NUMBER OF MEANS by which old corporations can launch new products using the mechanism of online and mobile communities. The first thing that the executives at the old corporations should do is to launch one brand, and not attempt to push a corporate identity program in these two new ecosystems where trust is critically important. Old corporations in many cases, and particularly among the millennials, have no bond of trust, but brands often have loyal fans.

Experiential Marketing

The following is the pitch of a communiteer to an established cosmetics manufacturer. With the success of the book and movie *The DaVinci Code*—40 million copies in print and $678 million in box office revenues—it is an established fact that people like to go on searches, to look for clues that lead to other clues and that finally produce a win. Let's take a brand, a skin care product for teenage girls, as the brand that we want to build a community around. We'll call it "FaceUp," as in "Face up to the truth: You can be great looking."

Now let's hide 100 tubes of FaceUp in secret places throughout the country. The hiding places will be in mobile phone stores, inside attractive cases that look like mobile phone carrying cases; but they are hidden within the stores such that even the clerks don't know that they are hidden there. The FaceUp community will be co-sponsored by one or more of the wireless carriers—Verizon, AT&T, Sprint, T-Mobile, and others—because they will benefit and because they will be needed to carry the content.

Prizes must be awarded to the girls who find the 100 makeup bags containing a bottle of FaceUp, and the prizes must be worth the effort—or, as it has been said, "The juice must be worth the squeeze." The announcement of the contest can be made via an ad on MySpace.com, with dates set for the follow-up announcements of 10 consecutive clues to be released at two- or three-week intervals on MySpace.com and on the new web site, FaceUp.com, the latter to be ported to contestants' mobile phones. When they log in they will give their e-mail address and their mobile phone number to FaceUp's parent. They will also opt in to receive clues directly from FaceUp.

Three things are gained by FaceUp in the early stages of the contest: (1) potential customers' e-mail addresses, (2) mobile phone numbers and (3) their willingness to receive text messages from FaceUp. A fourth thing is the beginning of an online community and a mobile community of teenage girls who could become loyal, trusting FaceUp customers.

Then the clues begin. They should follow the five fundamental points necessary to all successful communities:

1. *Art.* Use a lot of art and few words. The clues should involve art, which means museums, poetry, books, movies, theater, opera and music.
2. *Design.* The design of the FaceUp web site should be done by someone with the mind of a teenager and appear edgy and risky.
3. *Primitivism.* The clues should be read by rookies, not proven or experienced actors, because rookies are like teenagers—unproven, unremarkable, unknown.
4. *Games theory.* The clues should be such that they encourage collaboration with others in order to unravel the locations that hold subsequent clues. The wisdom of crowds trumps the expert working alone. The FaceUp web site should encourage girls to form groups

of strangers in order to decipher and untangle the clues more quickly.

5. *Keep quiet.* FaceUp's management should not talk to the media. The manufacturer of FaceUp should be a secret. If the teenagers know that a giant corporation is behind the contest, they may quit, because of general mistrust or a previous unsuccessful experience with another product from that manufacturer.

The FaceUp mobile and online communities should build rapidly, and there could be a mobbing effect until the 100 hidden bottles are found and prizes awarded.

Now, here is where it gets interesting: storytelling. Just as the prizes are awarded to the 100 winners, FaceUp announces that even bigger prizes—scholarships worth $10,000 a year for four years, for example—will be awarded to the individuals who write the best stories about their search for the hidden FaceUp bottles. In this way, FaceUp is encouraging user-generated content that can be used in future ads and can be printed in a FaceUp newsletter sent monthly to the e-mail addresses that have been captured. The winners of the essay contest should be judged by the users, again because it is user-generated data.

At the end, the manufacturer of FaceUp can ask if the mob that it has created would like to do it again, or would like to have an ad-writing contest for FaceUp, or would like FaceUp to brand other products, and if so, which ones, or if they would like to have another contest for a sister product three months or six months from now. In the meantime, FaceUp's marketing department can ping the mobile phone numbers of its mobile community members, by joint-venturing with Dodgeball and Buddy Ping, with a coupon, discount, twofer, tickets to a concert, airplane tickets or whatever to keep the buzz going among the members. *Unexpected rewards to members are sensational trust builders.*

To avoid destroying this new, carefully constructed relationship between the brand and the customers, it will be important to avoid placing ads for related products on the FaceUp web pages. Let the brand managers of the related products find their own solutions to reach out to the millennials. Your challenge after a successful experiential marketing program in which you created buzz, stir and recognition for the FaceUp brand is to keep the momentum going.

Keeping the Momentum Going

Ask yourself: Why would a teenage girl return to the FaceUp web site or community after the experience of the search and the storytelling is over? She has no reason to. The program was designed to launch the product and it was done well. To keep the buzz going, a second program is needed. Although there are several options to choose from, I would recommend some variation of the users group. The reasons are that teenagers want to be members of several groups at once—according to Rheingold's Law, teenagers want to expand their circle of friends to about 150; people are genetically wired to collaborate; and the FaceUp company can learn quite a bit about their consumers by listening in on their conversations (data mining, as it is called).

In addition, users groups have a dozen potential revenue channels which were described earlier. These include booth space rental, sponsorship fees (the wireless carriers owe FaceUp big-time!), subscriptions and ad space for a users group daily newspaper, admission, override on hotel rooms and on airplane seats, and revenues from T-shirts, caps and other miscellany.

The purpose of the users group (or trade show) is, as I see it, a recycling of two enormously successful business models—Mary Kay Ash's party-plan selling and Jean Nidetch's seminar selling. The subject of feminine beauty seems to be a topic of conversation at the point of sale, and the more opinions and give-and-take about one's attempts to be more beautiful, the more product can be sold. The FaceUp users group should combine those two models and be a moving seminar that goes to the teenagers—as they are not of driving age—and repeats the events in every major market for which area codes were gathered in phase one.

The exhibitors and sponsors should be carefully chosen. Although no products will actually be sold at the exhibitors' booths, quite a few badges will be swiped and names of teenage girls will be captured for future marketing purposes. FaceUp's wireless partners and MySpace.com will have to be given prime booth space, because they were helpful in the launch. Video game makers would zing and pop to the users group events, as would indie musicians, artists, designers and guest appearances by new male movie star wannabes, giving dating tips or just talking. The list of exhibitors could go on and on, but I think you get the point.

Be ever mindful to avoid banging the girls over the head with other brands, or hawking the users group meeting dates on TV or in print. Stick to the two communities you have built, plus your MySpace partnership. The wireless carriers should promote the users groups on their home pages as well, since they are selling more minutes than FaceUp is selling bottles of makeup. And above all, the FaceUp company should avoid talking to the media, bragging in trade magazines or congratulating their marketing team in public because it could break the bond of trust that the brand has established with the girls.

9

Foreign Exchange Market

EVERY NEW COLONY needs a means of payment: a currency. On the Internet, there are many currencies, and an entrepreneurial solution is needed to make the currencies interchangeable. The opportunity is to create and operate a "foreign exchange" market online and off-line where the following currencies can be exchanged for one another:

U.S. currency	Frequent stayer (hotel)
EU currency	points
UK currency	Frequent shopper points
Chinese currency	Prepaid phone card minutes
Japanese currency	"Slot club" (frequent gambler)
ATM balances	points
Credit/debit card	Mythical currency earned in
balances	Morpegs
Frequent flyer points	Kudos

Your new company will serve as a clearinghouse in cyberspace and in the off-line world that will enable anyone with a cell phone, PDA or PC with Internet access, located anywhere on earth, to exchange their form of currency for another form of currency in a matter of a few seconds.

You could charge a fee of 1 percent per transaction. If the volume of transactions rises to $10 billion per year, your company would be capable of doing $100 million in annual revenues.

IGE has a Morpeg Monopoly

Although it may seem strange to those who have not played Morpegs, there is currently an active foreign exchange market in currencies earned in the mythical worlds of Norrath in the Morpeg EverQuest II. It is inhabited by dwarfs, wizards and princesses. An active currency exchange market is operated by IGE at which mythical gold coins earned on Norrath are exchanged for U.S. or other real currencies, or vice versa. Such exchanges take place. Game makers Sony, Microsoft and others did not see this opportunity, but let others take it. This means, among other things, that Sony or Microsoft might back you in creating an online currency exchange business.

Edward Castronova, our leading student of the economics of Morpeg, observes the following:

> By now, no one in the synthetic world bats an eye over the idea that it might cost about 100 of EverQuest's platinum pieces to get one U.S. dollar . . . online auctions of game items begin to appear weeks in advance of the game's release.

EBay abandoned the business of managing an auction market for the exchange of synthetic items and currency in late January 2007 because, in the opinion of Rafat Ali, the editor of the widely read *Prepaid Content* newsletter, there was too much fraud.

If there is a foreign exchange market that will enable a myriad of currencies, both mythical and real, to be converted into cash, is it too far a stretch to conceive an exchange of all sorts of fungible assets from carbon emission credits to viatical insurance and from old magazines to bottles of wine? Bazaars, swap meets, pawn shops and derivative markets have been around for years. Moving them to an online community and porting the software to mobile phones would appear to be the next step.

Julian Dibbell makes an interesting point in his exceptional book, *Play Money: Or, How I Quit My Day Job and Made Millions Trading Virtual Loot*, that Karl Marx may be the economic inspiration for the age of trading mythical assets. Marx wrote in his *Communist Manifesto*, "All that is solid melts into air." Marx saw capitalism as a permanent revolution leaving nothing untouched in its constant, inexorable movement. It melts away everything that is solid in its inevitable rush to discard what exists and create its replacement. The result is dematerialization, and the creation of derivatives that represent those materials. Dibbell puts it this way: "Meanwhile, back in the marketplace, material goods themselves cede pride of place to brands, copyrights, patents, and other intangibles more central to the creation of wealth." In other words, rather than lament the outsourcing of the production of material assets to lowest cost producers, or the warming of the planet or the growth in viatical insurance in which the buyer bets on the death of a terminally ill person, one might view these problems as opportunities to create a highly liquid exchange marketplace in the derivatives that they create, such as temporary staffing, carbon emission credits and viatical policies.

To be sure, there are off-line markets in each of these categories and many more, but if Marx is right, and everything solid melts into air, and bits and bytes travel through the ether, then it is an ineluctable modality of the inevitable, to borrow a line from James Joyce, that the greatest marketplace for trading derivative assets will be online and mobile communities.

Starting a Currency Exchange Community

Let's look step-by-step at what it would take to launch this type of online or mobile-based business.

Begin with a Small Footprint

The business model for an ambitious company of this sort requires an experienced Wall Street *cage*, as it is referred to, where money and things convertible into money are exchanged—think of engaging Goldman Sachs & Company as a partner. Yet the initial model should be tested with one derivative and then, if it works, a second, and a third and so on can be added.

There are a handful of start-ups operating barter exchanges in old CDs, video games, books, DVDs, records, school books and magazines. Their revenue sources appear to be fee for service, although one of them, TitleTrader.com, charges a $19.95 annual subscription with no fee per transaction. The other online barter firms include Lala.com, Peerflix.com and Barterbee.com.

Since these four companies are competing for the business of closet cleaners, you might want to begin with carbon emission credits, or temporary staffing, which address much larger problems and will result in larger wealth creation, if your execution is as impeccable as eBay's.

A Necessary Unit of Value

Here's where it gets interesting. First, let's give your new company a name. Perhaps All Derivatives Exchange, or AllDex, will suffice. You will want an unimpeachable unit of value, plus insurance and reinsurance from AAA insurers to guarantee the constancy of that value. The gold standard once worked, but that was in an off-line world. You will want a unit of value that can be converted into any currency anywhere—commercial bank, ATM, stock brokerage, e-wallet or at the online foreign exchange market described earlier. In fact, with the existing ATM market clearly ready for entrepreneurial disruption—I mean, c'mon, ATMs should have been created to issue money orders or cashier's checks 20 years ago—you might think in terms of virtual ATM machines as the visual on your home page.

Strategic Alliances

AllDex is going to require launching with strong partners: a clearinghouse brokerage firm, an insurance carrier, a reinsurance carrier, a builder of an online currency exchange, mathematicians to value every conceivable derivative and a partner for many of the assets that will be bartered and swapped. If you begin with carbon emission credits, you might align yourself with the Chicago Climate Exchange, which trades carbon credits between carbon emitters and carbon reducers.

Web Portal-Based

The entrepreneur who seizes this opportunity will construct a Web portal. Let's call the company Fungible, Inc. and the Web portal Fungible.com. The Web portal can be constructed that will handle all currency exchanges using inputs of up-to-date, second-by-second bid and ask prices of all the "currencies." There are a number of builders of online auctions that Fungible's founders can hire for $100,000 to $200,000 to build the engine and create the pages. Kyle Gillman's team at ForgeFinder.com in Pittsburgh, Pennsylvania, is one that I have used successfully.

The Web portal Fungible.com will have a payment window to extract for Fungible.com a fee of 1 percent on each transaction from the seller. As an example, if a person has accumulated 50,000 "slot points" for gambling online and wants to convert them to cash and put them on her MasterCard, the software engine in the Web portal will observe that one slot point is worth, for example, one-tenth of a cent. The Web portal reaches out over P2P networks to all bidders, and asks people to match the lady's bid. The market clearing price is found in 60 seconds, and the lady is wired $49.50, after the deduction of a 50 cent fee.

But if the woman wants to convert the $50 to Palladium Gold Dust from the land of Norrath, Fungible.com's engine can do that as well. If it does not have any Palladium Gold Dust for sale from a seller, it will broadcast via blog or e-mail to its active traders the need for Palladium Gold Dust, and in several minutes, upon the arrival of the dust seller, it will effect the trade, when a market-clearing ask matches up to the bid. Fungible.com earns another 50 cents.

Probability of Success of Fungible.com

Holding the Fungible.com business model up to the test in Chapter 5, let's attempt to score it. First, the size of the problem, or P, is extraordinarily large. All of us collect points on airlines, at bookstores, at hotels, on our credit cards and so forth, and we need a clearinghouse to convert them to cash or to put money into our credit cards, or to buy mythical property on SecondLife or on EverQuest II. I would rate P a 3.

The solution, or S, of holding a continual auction for points, mythical money and all of the major currencies online, and porting it to a mobile community in order to make purchases or sales on the fly, appears to me to be simple, and therefore other, more likely candidates can create a Fungible.com, such as Citigroup or BancAmerica, but haven't considered doing it. However, it probably cannot be patented or protected from copycatting, and thus cannot be given a 3. I would give the S factor a score of 2.75.

The entrepreneurial team, or E factor, will clearly need a leader who is the Nureyev of banking and foreign exchange, a Baryshnikov of auction engines and a Makarova of strategic alliance builders. If this team of experienced performers can be assembled, I would place a score of 3 on the E factor. I envision a world of online and mobile communities in which points and mythical currencies are awarded in a symphonic rhythm that moves harmoniously in tandem with the growth and development of Fungible.com to convert real money to points and mythical currencies, and vice versa. "If you build it, they will come," as James Earl Jones said to Kevin Costner in the movie *Field of Dreams*. This certainly applies to Fungible.com.

Now, for the DEJ factors, see Table 9.1. Fungible.com, I believe, scores a perfect 8 in DEJ factors.

TABLE 9.1   Fungible.com: Demonstrable Economic Justification Test

DEJ Factor	Ask	What Will It Cost?
1. Existence of qualified buyers	Are the consumers to whom a foreign exchange auction market will be marketing aware that they need the service?	Advertising in the form of persuading alliance partners such as the airlines and Morpeg publishers will be needed. Relatively modest cost because the alliance partners will benefit. Games makers could invest in Fungible.com because it enhances the liquidity of their markets tremendously.
2. Large number of buyers	Are there lots of consumers who need this service?	There are 110 million Morpeg players, 75 million holders of frequent flyer points, 45 million holders of frequent stayer (hotels) points and hundreds of millions of people who will earn mythical points on the communities that will soon be created.
3. Homogeneity of buyers	Will the market accept a standardized service or will the service need to be customized?	One size fits all. No customizing cost.
4. Existence of competent sellers	Is the service so complex to explain that customers will be leery of it, and need time to understand it before using Fungible.com?	Morpeg players are using IGE's exchange market auction at a growing rate. The path has been laid out by IGE. No cost.

(Continued)

TABLE 9.1 *(Continued)*

DEJ Factor	Ask	What Will It Cost?
5. Lack of institutional barriers to entry	Is there a requirement for government or institutional approval in order to tap into this market?	None. There is no cost, only an e-wallet system to move currencies—mythical and real—and points through this new ecosystem.
6. Ease of promotion by word of mouth	Can the merits of Fungible.com's service be passed from one person to another?	Yes. It is the type of service that people will describe with the same joy with which they discuss wine, travel, movies, restaurants and music.
7. Invisibility of the inside of the company	Is there a need to reveal profits or the business model to the public?	None. Fungible.com can remain private for several years and capture massive market share before its IPO.
8. Optimum price/cost relationship	Is the selling price of the service substantially above cost of revenues?	Yes. The model is similar to that of eBay: Create an auction engine and secure it tightly. The algorithms will do 99 percent of the work. Capital expenditures for servers and security systems could run $1–2 million. Developing or licensing an e-wallet system from GenieBancor.com or another vendor will represent a cost per transaction, but not an upfront cost.

As for the "Float Many Clubs" factors, I can visualize an initial start-up cost of about $1.5 million for capital expenditures as follows:

Designing the web portal	$100,000
Designing the auction engine	$100,000
Servers, security system	$ 50,000
Salaries for skunkworks designers	$100,000
Travel, communications to convince strategic partners to join	$ 50,000
Legal, consulting, accounting to develop contracts, billing systems, payment systems and accounting systems	$150,000
Up-front design of the e-wallet platform	$100,000
Working capital to pay salaries and benefits, plus rent, utilities, broadband, transportation and other operating expenses for 12 months or until breakeven is attained	$800,000
Miscellaneous and working capital reserve	$ 50,000
Total start-up budget	**$1,500,000**

There is no float for Fungible.com in the traditional sense of having customers prepay. However, Fungible.com removes a liability from the balance sheets of airlines and creates enormous liquidity for morpeg players. Thus, the corporations that fly passengers and sell video games stand to gain so handsomely that they are likely to invest in Fungible.com through their corporate venture capital subsidiaries. Delta Airlines made a handsome return on its investment in Priceline.com and Microsoft did well on its investment in Audible, Inc. Combining their capital with $500,000 from Benchmark Capital, the venture capital fund that backed eBay and that knows this space, is the route I would take.

The "many" factor addresses marketing through associations and affinity groups. I would approach the communities that aggregate frequent travelers such as Facebook.com and SecondLife.com. If Sony, Microsoft or Electronic Arts seek to enhance the liquidity of the Morpeg community, they should be willing to lease their customers' e-mail addresses on a one-shot basis to start a buzz going. Airlines could be persuaded to put a flyer for Fungible.com into their monthly mailers. Hotel and motel chains might do so as well.

The "clubs" factor might evolve like this. A forum would be created on one of the pages on the Fungible.com Web portal. Users would be encouraged to discuss their experiences, provide suggestions to improve the system, and report defectors who try to launder drug money through the

TABLE 9.2 Fungible.com: Three-Month Cash Flow Statement, Post-Launch

	Month 1	Month 2	Month 3
Number of customers	1,300,000	1,950,000	2,600,000
Revenues $0.50 per transaction	$ 650,000	$ 975,000	$1,300,000
Cost of revenues			
License fee for e-wallet at 5 percent	32,500	48,750	65,000
Salaries of auction engine personnel—five at $75,000/year	40,000	40,000	40,000
Total cost of revenues	72,500	88,750	105,000
Gross Profit	577,500	886,250	1,195,000
Operating expenses			
Management salaries: three at $150,000/year each	50,000	50,000	50,000
Salaries of support staff: five at $40,000/year each	12,000	12,000	12,000
Marketing expense-blogging, SEOs, rentals, etc.	130,000	195,000	260,000
Travel, communications, marketing support	25,000	30,000	35,000
Other expenses (rent, utilities, etc.)	50,000	50,000	50,000
Miscellaneous, supplies, couriers, bank charges	25,000	25,000	25,000
Total operating expenses	292,000	362,000	432,000
Net operating income	285,500	524,250	763,000

marketplace. In the forum, users will converse with one another to enhance the utility of the public good that Fungible.com will grow to become. Clubs within users may form, as they have formed on Wikipedia. Wikipedia has a regulating group, an arbitration committee to rule on disputes and the mediation committee made up of 14 Wikipedians authorized to trace I.P. addresses in cases of suspected abuse. These groups grew organically and have been beneficial to Wikipedia's public "goodness." The same is likely to occur at Fungible.com, if people enjoy the benefits and seek to maintain them.

The resulting score that I get for Fungible.com is 42. That is huge.

What are Fungible.com's likely monthly revenues shortly after launch? Let's assume optimal cooperation from three airlines and all Morpeg producers, so that 130 million people are made aware of their opportunity to convert an unused currency into a useful currency. Further, assume that 1 percent of this universe conducts one trade worth $50 in one month after launch, that 1.5 percent conduct one trade worth $50 in month two and that 2 percent conduct one trade worth $50 in month three. Table 9.2 on the previous page is a three-month cash flow statement projection for Fungible.com immediately following the launch.

Because a fee is earned on each trade, Fungible.com will not have to wait for revenues to become cash. Thus, net operating income is equal to cash flow.

Summary

The complexity in launching Fungible.com is in the details prior to launch. The entrepreneurial team must be experienced in conventional foreign exchange operations, auction engine development and maintenance and negotiating strategic alliances. The utility offered by the service is quite ubiquitous and easy to explain, thus marketing and buzz building should not be a major challenge. Because Fungible.com is a public good, the users must be encouraged to continually improve on the model, and get involved in reputation management.

10

The Metaverse
Arbitration Association

OFF-LINE COURTS ARE CROWDED. Justice delayed is justice denied. A new
judicial system is needed to settle disputes that occur in online and mobile communities. A reputation management system is effective to a
point, but it needs the teeth of a judiciary to punish those who take advantage of the public goods. As Dr. Strangelove said in Stanley Kubrick's
1963 movie, "Deterrence is necessary to produce fear in the hearts of the
perpetrators." The deterrence mechanism will not be imprisonment,
but rather the publication of the rulings of the Metaverse Arbitration
Association.

The Model

The 80-year-old American Arbitration Association (AAA) handles
more than 50,000 cases each year. It draws on the services of approximately 10,000 arbitrators, many of whom are experts in a particular business or industry. The AAA recently expanded into Europe, where it
handled 600 dispute resolution cases last year. In February 2006, the
Supreme Court of the United States handed down their opinion in
Buckeye Check Cashing v. Cardegna, which came down strongly in favor

of using arbitration to resolve a wide range of disputes. An AAA arbitrator, thus, has the authority to enter a binding, court-enforceable judgment from which only the most limited kind of appeal is allowed. The fee for filing an AAA arbitration request from $1.00 up to $10,000 is $700. There are further fees along the way, such as paying for the arbitrator's time.

I envision that all communities will be encouraged, through an association of online and mobile communities (described in Chapter 27), to have their subscribers sign an agreement that all future disputes will be resolved by arbitration. The following language in the contract is recommended:

> In the event of any dispute between you and others on this site, you and the others agree to resolve the dispute through the auspices of the Metaverse Arbitration Association in (City-State). Any award rendered shall be final and conclusive upon the parties. The prevailing party shall be entitled to his costs in connection with such arbitration and the enforcement thereof.

The Size of the Problem

Online and mobile communities are public goods, like whales and Little League baseball fields, and must be sustained and protected by their members or else, sadly, governments will intervene. Social networks fill a big need for people of all ages and stages of life, and they run the risk of becoming antisocial networks.

The Yamanner worm struck Yahoo's web mail server in June 2006 when a virus writer sent out an e-mail with some Java Script code invisibly inside it. Anyone opening an e-mail triggered the script which requested the user's address book and then sent the worm to everyone listed. Developers of malware—short for "malicious software"—can enter the coding of Java Script and change it to capture names for spam purposes. Mash-ups are particularly vulnerable, because programmers combine applications, as could occur, for instance, with Google's ads placed near relevant words in MySpace profiles.

Further, there are cheaters in online games. They are known as *griefers* because they cause grief to the players. There are decoys—pseudonymous names representing corporations trying to push their brands. Finally, there are sexual predators and their acts are criminal and beyond the scope of arbitration to solve. And, finally there are sellers who do not receive mythical goods that they purchase from buyers, and buyers who get stiffed by sellers of mythical goods.

The problems are both security and defectors. Security is usually handled after the fact by developers, but many start-ups lack the capital to protect their Web servers. They will be the most vulnerable to attacks. Defectors can be handled less expensively and more quickly by the Metaverse Arbitration Association (MAA). The problem has an indeterminate size. Do 10 percent of all members of a community attempt to jump the turnstile? Or is it 20 percent? Without deterrence, the problem will grow.

The Elegance of the Solution

With conventional judicial systems overcrowded and unwilling, thus far, to deal with disputes that occur in online communities, the door is wide open—so wide open, you could drive a Mack truck through it—to launch the MAA. Moreover, there is a perfectly wonderful off-line model: the AAA.

The Entrepreneurial Team

Hiring a senior officer from CyberSettle, an online arbitration organization founded in 1996, or AAA could be key to your successful launching of the MAA. Other criteria in assembling a team will include sales and marketing to spread the word to all communities. A second player will be someone to convince lawyers to participate as arbitrators. Since lawyers frequently visit their bar associations' web sites to sign up for courses, establishing links on these web sites will be helpful.

There are no institutional barriers to entering this business. The media will be helpful; it's the kind of story they like. They will help word-of-mouth to spread. The market is aware of the need, and will not have to be educated with advertising. The settling of disputes and the payment of awards to complainants will be proof that the MAA works. Without that, the MAA could die. Therefore, prelaunch beta-testing will be a good idea. Communities will have to place banners on their home pages stating that they are sponsors of the MAA.

The MAA does not disrupt a traditional industry, but, rather, it solves pain. The courts do not want to handle online disputes; lawyers who become MAA arbitrators can earn extra income; and complainants can resolve their disputes using MAA rapidly and without much cost. It's a win-win-win.

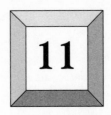

Rent a Judge

THE METAVERSE ARBITRATION ASSOCIATION will need judges. If the MAA is created as a dot-org (.org), a not-for-profit company, its creator can subcontract a dot-com company to generate a steady flow of attorneys and trial judges to service the disputes brought before the MAA.

The Temporary Staffing Business

The U.S. or UK off-line temporary staffing industry serves as an excellent model for what I will call RentAJudge.com. The industry is projected to be worth $133 billion in the United States. The staffing companies are paid by the corporations, generally at a premium, and they pay their workers 20 to 30 percent less than they receive. Thus, their gross profit margins average around 20 to 30 percent.

In the MAA model, payment to RentAJudge.com will come from the parties to the dispute. Assume that a judge hearing an MAA dispute bills at an hourly rate of $300 and estimates that the dispute in question will require three hours of his time. RentAJudge.com would bill the MAA around $1,000 and earn $300 gross profit. If more time is needed, the judge will so indicate to the MAA, and there will be a subsequent billing.

Maintaining High Standards

At the end of each dispute, the parties will be asked to rate the judges. RentAJudge.com will maintain the scores and use them in making future recommendations to disputants. One judge might be very good at settling disputes concerning the purchase and sale of property in mythical worlds but not be as successful at settling disputes arising from foreign exchange transfers. Eventually, the rating system will enable RentAJudge.com to make the best placements.

What Entrepreneurial Skills Are Needed?

A strong sales and marketing team will be needed to find lawyers and retired judges to enter their names and resumes into a pool of available arbitrators. Bar associations may be persuaded to provide links on their web sites to RentAJudge.com. The bar associations may want to be paid an advertising fee, and that is understandable, because outside of their courses, they have no other meaningful revenue streams. As long as the fee is small, such as 5 percent of the placement fee for each of their members that is placed by RentAJudge.com, they should be paid. After all, the bars serve the additional role of endorsers.

Hungry lawyers can be located through law school alumni associations. They will gladly participate, because they will be aiding the cause of recent graduates who have just hung out their shingles and are seeking clients. They represent low-hanging fruit to the RentAJudge.com marketing squad.

RentAJudge.com will need to assist the MAA in obtaining disputants. With 110 million people playing Morpegs, one might assume that there are at least 100,000 disputes a year concerning property transfers. Placing a link on the home pages of the tens of thousands of games, and in the online magazines, such as CheaterPlant, could persuade 10 percent of the gamers who feel cheated to file complaints with the MAA.

Using the $1,000 fee mentioned earlier as a standard, RentAJudge.com could realize first-year revenues of 10,000 × $1,000, or $10 million and a gross profit of $7 million. Even if the bar associations are paid 5 percent of the gross, or $500,000, the balance of $6.5 million is a tidy sum. This little business could become a cash cow to its founders.

What Are the Start-Up Costs?

This start-up will need a web site design for $100,000 to $150,000 and three entrepreneurs: Two will make the sales calls and one will operate the data management and search engine to match arbitrators with disputes. Support staff will be needed to continually update and improve the Web portal and search engine as well as the rating system. The Web portal will require a forum page with an FAQ section and a consumer and judge comment section. RentAJudge.com must be highly transparent, because the media will be watching the site constantly to look for flaws. "If it bleeds, it leads," as they say in journalistic circles, and bad news about RentAJudge.com will travel faster than Olympic downhill skiers.

Assuming three entrepreneurs and a staff of seven in supporting roles, a monthly burn rate (including communications, travel, server purchases, rent and utilities) of $84,000, and positive breakeven attained in the seventh month, RentAJudge.com will require an estimated 6 × $84,000, or $504,000, to launch. You had better raise $600,000 to be safe.

If revenues from the 7th to the 18th month are $10 million and the gross profit after payments to the bars is $6.5 million, the operating costs of $84,000 per month or $1.008 million, could be easily paid. The net profits to stockholders would be around $5.5 million before taxes, which would be somewhat blunted by the first six months of losses.

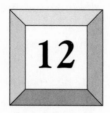

Publishing and Convention Management

THE OPPORTUNITY TO LAUNCH new paper magazines and trade shows to service the forthcoming explosion of communities and colonies is so big that the entrepreneur who launches the top trade show for community founders and managers could be, in the words of the philosopher Yogi Berra, creating "déjà vu all over again" when it is compared with Comdex.

There are going to be tens of thousands of online communities, and many of them will be coming together for the first time to discuss common problems and issues that affect them. They will need a *service* magazine (or newsletter). A service magazine is one that services the peculiar needs of a certain affinity group.

Trade shows are living magazines—the booth space represents the ads and the seminars represent the text. There are at least 11 substantial cash flow business models in the trade show business:

1. Fee charged to attendees.
2. Booth space rentals to exhibitors.

3. Sponsorships: providers of lanyards to carry the attendees' names imprinted on plastic and inserted into a clear plastic window; backpacks or tote bags; books listing exhibitors, booth space and speakers; the ubiquitous coffee mug and a notepad with built-in pen.
4. Ads in the trade show daily newspaper.
5. Books containing transcripts of seminars.
6. CDs containing transcripts of the seminars.
7. An override on hotel rooms in the city that hosts the trade show.
8. An override on airplane seats that transport the attendees to the trade show.
9. Sales of T-shirts, caps, posters, telephone pads and other miscellany.
10. Renting the IP addresses of attendees to hardware and software manufacturers.
11. Market research gathered from attendees repurposed as consulting studies sold to old corporations that seek to create communities as a social network around their products.

Business Model for Communiteer Expo

Let's give this business a name. How about Communiteer Expo, which can be shortened to TeerEx once some traction is achieved.

Now let's make the following assumptions:

Number of first-year attendees	5,000
Entrance fee	$200
Fee from first-year sponsors	$75,000 (each)
Number of exhibitor booths	200
Price per booth	$5,000
Number of ads in trade show daily	10 × 3 days
Average price of each ad	$3,000
Number of unit sales of T-shirts, caps, etc.	1,000
Average price of a T-shirt, etc.	$25.00
Other revenue channels	(none at first TeerEx)

Calculation of First-Year Revenues

Attendees	$1,000,000
Sponsors	225,000
Exhibitor booths	100,000
Ads in trade show daily	90,000
T-shirts, caps, etc.	25,000
Total Revenues	**$1,440,000**

Cost of Goods Sold

The conference rooms of a hotel in a fairly large city—a minimum of 5,000 available "pillows," as they say in the tourism industry—will have to be rented for four days, which includes one day for setting up and three days for the convention. Surprisingly, the cost is lower than you think, because hotels bid aggressively for trade shows. They prefer "computer types," as they have told me, "because they spend more money more freely than doctors or lawyers," who can rent the conference rooms and exhibit hall for $10,000 a day, or about $50,000 with set-up and janitorial services. This cost is higher in heavily unionized cities, such as Chicago, where the labor costs are higher.

With sponsors prepaying their sponsorships, you should have $225,000 in free float without cost of goods sold from the cups, badge holders and tote bags. There is no cost of goods sold for the booth space, either. Assume that the ads in the trade show daily pay for the entire print budget—three days of trade show daily, exhibitors' directory, badges, banners and the staff to check visitors into the show—a total of about $90,000. Then assume that the T-shirts and caps have a 50 percent cost of goods sold ratio. The total revenues less cost of goods sold would appear as follows:

Revenues	$ 1,440,000
Cost of goods sold	140,000
Gross profit	**$1,300,000**

Operating Costs

Let's assume you do virtually all of your advertising on the Internet. You use the network effect—that is, decision influencers are given free passes or persuaded to put news of the show on their blogs. The blogs direct readers to come to your web site to get all the information about the trade show and to preregister if they wish (more float). You search-engine-optimize (SEO) the show on Google, Yahoo! and the 14 other search engines. And you e-mail and snail-mail the founders of all online communities, urging them to come to this event along with members of their staff to share ideas with fellow communiteers. Let's estimate an advertising budget of $100,000.

Finally, you will need to line up some top speakers and pay their fees (if any) along with travel, room and board, and you will need to create a booth for your company and staff it during the show. Put another $100,000 into operating expenses. Toss in another $40,000 for insurance, legal and miscellaneous, and operating expenses come to $240,000. The trade show's first-year operating statement budget looks something like the following:

Revenues	$ 1,440,000
Cost of goods sold	(140,000)
Gross profit	1,300,000
Operating expenses	(240,000)
Net profit	**$1,060,000**

That's a tidy sum, and sufficient to expand the advertising and marketing to double the size of the next show and to double it again in the third year.

The trade show business is highly scalable. If 10,000 visitors attend and there are 600 exhibitor booths and five sponsors, costs do not increase proportionately. Thus, three years out, when revenues have grown to more than $5 million, the show should earn more than $3.5 million. And you, as a producer, will have the respect of the community of communiteers to publish the industry's principal trade magazine.

13

Taking Back
the Automobile Market

To DEMONSTRATE THE POWER of communiteering to disrupt economies, I suggest that we turn its power around to bring back General Motors, Ford and DaimlerChrysler to their once proud status of the top three automakers in the world. We'll call this site ReinventingCars.com.

A brave communiteer will ask the crowds to display their wisdom for remaking the country's three largest auto and truck manufacturers by contributing ideas and drawings. The ideas could range from redesigning cars and trucks to redesigning their business models. As mentioned earlier, automakers are spending more money on TV ads for their products while TV viewership steadily declines. See Figure 14.1 on page 178. This peculiar behavior—comparable to setting one's hair on fire and trying to put it out with a hammer—needs to be stopped. How might the crowds come up with an alternative?

The crowds might suggest slashing the TV ad budget by 80 to 90 percent to free up cash for redeveloping the GM, Ford and Chrysler models. Some of the billions of dollars of freed-up cash can then be redeployed to online and mobile communities. There are numerous means for spending money with communiteers, as we have seen. These include experiential marketing, as Audi did with its A2 model; tip jars paid to car and truck designers who come up with the best ideas, as voted on by the members; kudos awarded by the manufacturers themselves with the kudos being applied to new car purchases; facilities management contracts awarded to the community's owner for managing the community; multilevel marketing dollars paid to members by the manufacturers for bringing in new customers; a reverse auction supply chain management subgroup within the community that controls vendor prices on all components that go into making cars and trucks; and user group fees whereby members pay for the right to join interior and exterior design clubs within the community that examine every single aspect of the Big Three with the goal of fixing or improving them.

The Dashboard as a New Media Carrier

The area that interests me the most is converting the dashboard to a PDA or mobile phone. I drive to and from work like many of you, and it is illegal in my state to hold my mobile phone to my ear while driving. But it would be legal to have a PDA on my dashboard programmed with the information that I would like to receive while driving. For safety purposes, much of this information would need to be aural rather than visual.

Radio signals have been beamed to cars and trucks for quite some time. A data-mining chip can be inserted into a radio that "knows" what I want to hear and when I want to hear it. Incoming e-mails and IMs can be sent to me in large type or converted to voice. My favorite blogs can be broadcast to me.

As the content publishers, the Big Three automakers can begin earning revenues by morphing from cars as vehicles to cars as content carriers. They can charge for the modified set-top box. They can share in carrier revenue minutes, and in WiMAX communities they can act as the carrier itself. They can share, through dividend distributions, in revenues earned by the community companies they invest in. And if the community companies they invest in go public or are acquired, they can profit through capital gains.

Let's run some numbers. Set-top boxes cost about $100 apiece to make and can be sold as retrofits for $300, with every imaginable feature, and $200 for the standard issue. The same prices can be used when the boxes are installed at the factory.

Let's assume that the average user burns 20 hours a week listening to his individualized dashboard PDA, and runs up a bill of $20 a week, or $1,000 per year. Of that amount, assume the automakers keep 50 percent, or $500 per year.

From these two revenue channels, the automakers have found $650 a year. If 1 million people buy the dashboard PDA and use it as much as I have suggested in year one, the automakers will have generated $650 million in new cash flow. At 5 million users, the cash flow becomes $3.25 billion, which begins to be considerable, given the current combined losses of the Big Three of about $17 billion a year.

Now, if they can save another $3 billion in TV advertising budget reductions, $1 billion in print advertising reductions and another $1 billion in vendor cost reductions via the reverse auction that the community runs for vendors, we have generated $8.25 billion in new cash flow for GM, Ford and DaimlerChrysler.

The buzz from the success of ReinventingCars.com could push up sales of the Big Three by 20 percent—particularly if designs improve, and the cars and trucks are more save-the-planet sensitive. Increased sales from buzz should bring another $5 billion to the bottom line. And, voila, the problem is fixed.

14

Mission Statement Rewriting

THE ONE THING WE CAN ALL AGREE ON when it comes to large consumer products and service companies is that they are slow to recognize and adapt to change. Entrepreneurs have been disrupting them for years. And for years, centuries in fact, big corporations have scoffed at entrepreneurial start-ups, only to see their customers flee to the start-ups.

This time the disruption will be cataclysmic. Major consumer products and services companies that have carpet bombed us with ads in print and visual media for more than a century will be radically disrupted.

Consumer behavior is miles ahead of the mind-set of the executives of consumer products marketers. Let's consider the automotive sector. The entrenched dealership organization blocks a transition to online marketing and prevents the IT departments of auto manufacturers from designing Web-based marketing models. Thus, the disruptions in this market will most likely come from entrepreneurs.

Automakers invested 50 percent of their advertising dollars in TV ads while consumers report that their purchase decisions are impacted only 27 percent by what they see on TV and more by what they learn via the Internet and in newspapers. See Figure 14.1.

Creative people in consumer products firms have gotten used to the 30-second spot as a vehicle for creating brand value and emotional appeal. But with the penetration of broadband into many homes and

Automakers overspend on television and magazine ads (as shown in the bar at left), underestimating the attention consumers pay to newspapers and the Internet (at right).

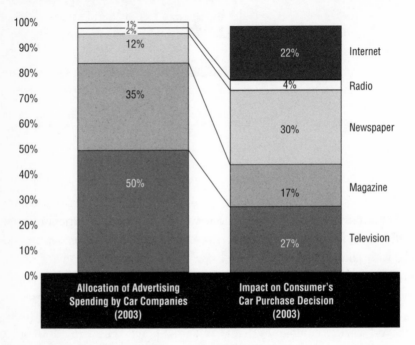

FIGURE 14.1 Waste in the Auto Advertising Media Mix
Source: CNW Research, as reported in *Strategy+Business,* "The Future of Advertising Is Now," August 15, 2006.

businesses, the opportunities to mash up interactive entertainment with advertising are immense. And the GPS chip inserted into many mobile phones—which could become ubiquitous as a counterbalance to increased homeland terrorism—means that the consumer can be reached at the point of purchase.

Coke Music

The Coca-Cola Company isn't sitting on its duff waiting to have its brand disrupted by entrepreneurs. It recently launched an online community where members sign in and create their own ringtones. It is a similar model to that of Sonic Branding Solutions, but Coke Music is online and Sonic's is mobile. I signed up at www.CokeMusic.com and created a tune. The revenue model is interesting. I could listen to the tunes of other members, and if I liked them I could send kudos, chits of praise. The kudos collected by the nascent Mozarts are currency, usable to purchase Coca-Cola products.

There are some flaws in Coke Music, such as more top-down management than entrepreneurial online and mobile communities put into their worlds. The web site design is tight and boxy, rather than open and primitive. But give Coca-Cola credit: It has begun to rethink branding and emotional awareness.

The word *thirst* is big on the Coke Music site. The creators seem to be attempting to link thirst for a cool coke and thirst for music. That's a good idea, along the lines of other consumer marketers that are reducing their brands' adjectival phrases to one word—for example, Lincoln Financial Group's *Hello Future*, Royal Bank of Scotland's *Action* and Apple Inc.'s *Innovation*.

Nine Ways to Launch a New Product in the Age of Communiteers

If you are going to rewrite mission statements for giant consumer marketers, here are nine new ways to market using online and mobile communities:

1. *Blog marketing.* Use RSS to push "feeds of me" where they can be collected by de.licio.us and Flickr.
2. *Experiential marketing.* Create an experience for community members whom you want to reach.
3. *Branded entertainment.* In storytelling communities, invite the members to incorporate your brand, or invent a new brand for you; make "user-branded" the new Good Housekeeping Seal of Approval.
4. *Mobile marketing.* Reach out to the opted-in mobile phone community member when he is standing in front of your product with several purchasing options; issue a coupon or twofer.

5. *Games with prizes*. Provide clues, then offer a prize for the winner who finds your products hidden somewhere that the clues lead to.

6. *On-demand viewing*. Forget prime time and think "my time." Let the viewer decide when he wants to view your launch.

7. *Social networking*. Create a community that deals with a subject of vital interest to people whom you would like to make customers of your company, and reward them for bringing customers to your company. Use tactics from multilevel marketing; for example, invite students to bring online customers to your company and give free tuition to those who bring you 95 new customers.

8. *Numbers of experiences*. Ad impressions no longer mean anything; don't bother counting them. The new measure is number of experiences—games, searches, opportunities to brand, ringtone games. Why can't your ad become a ringtone?

9. *The secret launch*. Hide new products somewhere; give 150 prizes to people who find them. Encourage the searchers to tell their search stories on a community site that you put up for this purpose. Give significant prizes for the best stories.

15

Mocketeering

IF ONE OF your goals is to enjoy some merry schadenfreude while operating a business, you will enjoy running the Mocketeering.com community. The business model of Mocketeering is to bring together funny people and designers to cooperatively work on reconstructing the packaging and the ads of consumer product and service companies. The collective effort should produce some wonderful ads, and the community can be constructed in such a manner that when the package or the ad is finished, the designers can offer it for sale, through the community, to the large corporation and quote a price for it. If purchased, the designers would keep, say, 80 percent of the sale price and the community 20 percent. Chevrolet would be an excellent first customer, as it goofed up on its attempt to develop user-generated ads for its 2007 Tahoe SUV.

"Mere entertainment becomes art when the communicative element in the work is either novel or exceptionally well done," writes Raph Koster in his delightful book, A *Theory of Fun for Game Design*. He continues, "And it's hard to imagine a medium more powerful in that regard than video games, where you are presented with interactivity and a virtual world that reacts to your choices."

Thus, if Koster is right—and who would question the developer of Ultima Online, a $500 million revenue-producing Morpeg that he produced while head of Sony Online—then the two fundamentals underlying Mocketeering.com should be games and sharing. Let's say a person subscribes to Mocketeering.com for $20 per year and develops a new ad for Gatorade. She puts her first draft up on the Mocketeering forum and asks for comments, critiques and changes. Dozens, perhaps hundreds, of changes and edits come in, and she modifies her ad, drawing the best from the bunch and puts it back up on the forum page. It may receive more changes, and if so they might be made. When it's finally set in stone, she sends tip-jar money to those advisers who helped her the most.

The mocketeered Gatorade ad in final form is copyrighted in the name of the subscriber and sent to Gatorade's advertising agency. The proper noncircumvention agreement accompanies the ad, although that is likely to be unnecessary, because consumer marketers that defect, or refuse to cooperate, will see their names published in the Mocketeering reputation management section.

The owners of Mocketeering.com will negotiate the price of the ad with Gatorade. When payment arrives, it is shared 80 percent with the Mocketeering ad designer and 20 percent with Mocketeering.com. If the ad brings in a price of $100,000, the ad designer receives $80,000 and Mocketeering.com receives $20,000.

Assuming 150,000 people subscribe to Mocketeering.com at $20 per annum in the first year, the Company will have float to work with of $3 million. If 20 ads are sold in year one for an average ticket of $100,000, Mocketeering will earn another $400,000. That's an excellent beginning for any start-up.

Moreover, the successful ad designers will earn $80,000 apiece, and for those who sell multiple ads, Mocketeering could generate real money for them.

The Tip-Jar Method of Sharing

"Collective decisions are most likely to be good ones when they're made by people with diverse opinions reaching independent conclusions, relying primarily on their private information," writes John Surowiecki in

The Wisdom of Crowds. The best ads for Gatorade or any other consumer product or service will probably be made by a crowd of people, each working independently.

Thus, the contributors to the winning Mocketeer ads should be rewarded by the ad designer who earns the $80,000 award from the advertising agency. Payments to the contributing designers should be made to their independent tip jars, without Mocketeering.com taking a finder's fee.

What will be interesting to watch evolve will be the minimum payment requirements that each contributor tapes onto the front of his tip jar. A $50 minimum would not be an unexpected posting for a first-time contributor to a successful Mocketeer ad, and that price could increase five- or tenfold with a second successful contribution. The ad designers would also rate the contributors and vice versa, using various criteria; but the telling sign of a contributor's true worth will be the minimum acceptable payment pasted onto his or her tip jar.

Calls from Fortune's 500

Mocketeering.com could become such a big hit that consumer product giants might begin contacting Mocketeering.com's management and asking to have their ads designed by the start-up. That scenario could get very interesting. Clearly the job requests will have to be valued and put out to the community on requests for proposals (RFPs), and there could be more fascinating bidding action. Some designers may be so confident in their ability to handle certain RFPs magnificently that they underbid the job. Other designers may call in their favorite contributors to jointly bid on the RFP. It could get crazy, as auctions often do. See Shlomo Matail's fascinating book *Economic Games People Play* to learn why people overbid at auctions.

Mocketeering.com would be entitled to a fee on jobs that come to the community from advertisers. A slice of 20 percent seems about right, because the company will have to build an auction engine to manage the bidding on the RFPs.

The Start-Up Process

Mocketeering.com will not be a difficult or costly community to launch. One of the most prolific builders of online communities is OneSite.com, based in Oklahoma City. It built over 300 of them in 2006 and has a backlog, including radio stations owned by Clear Channel Communications. Building the Mocketeering.com site will cost around $100,000, plus travel, room and board to Madison Avenue to convince a few advertising agencies to reach out to the wisdom of crowds for the publicity value of it—in addition, possibly more emotionally cryptic ads would cost another $25,000 or thereabouts.

Getting the first subscriber and convincing him to pay $20, and then getting the second, the third and so forth is where the rubber hits the road. Viral marketing is probably the way to go. This means persuading decision influencers with the best blogs to recommend Mocketeering. Winning a first advertising agency client willing to beta-test your premise will be useful. Then letting the media in on the success of the first project, if the consumer products market accepts the mob-developed design, will probably boost Mocketeering.com's membership into the tens of thousands.

An angel round of $200,000 is all the capital you will need to launch Mocketeering.com. It should earn ten times that amount in year one, and much more thereafter. Since Mocketeering.com can be replicated by many others, you are advised to talk very little about Mocketeering.com, or if you have to, discuss the difficulties of working with so many creative people, lawyers (the very word keeps competitors away) and the U.S. copyright office. Let them see you sweat. If photographed by the media, wear old clothes and scuffed shoes with torn and knotted laces. Appear poor because it blocks litigious lawyers who, upon seeing your inability to afford new shoelaces, will merely send you an "eat crap and die"s letter.

Launching a New Hotel Chain
Through an Online Community

USER-GENERATED DESIGN of an occupant's stay at a new hotel chain—
call it Millennial Hotels—can be done in a number of ways. My inspiration comes from several sources. First, the Finnish company Sulake
created a virtual community called Habbo Hotel (www.Habbo.com)
in which the visitor checks in and selects various design elements
from the database to create her environment. She pays Habbo for each
design element selected. She invites her friends to see the environment that she created, and this brings new members to Habbo Hotel.
The community reports that it now has 7.1 million members, mostly
Europeans. In several instances, Europeans are the primary disrupters
of existing industries; for example, Skype (Estonia), Sulake (Finland)
and HI5 (Spain).

The success of Habbo Hotel is based on the fun of designing one's
own environment in a virtual world. The act of *design* itself, according to
Daniel H. Pink in his book *A Whole New Mind*, has become more important to today's millennials—the generation that grew up on the Internet—than text. And the third leg of Habbo's success, I believe, is
user-generated content. Fun, design, and user-generated content spell
success.

Millennial Hotels can draw on these three factors to provide the occupants of its hotels with an exceptional experience that imitates the virtual experience of visiting Habbo Hotel: fun, design, user-generated content.

The second part of my launch plan is addressing the all important question: How do I get the first person to pay for my new service, and how do I get him to do to it a second time and to tell others about it? I have some ideas for that, primarily in the area of strategic alliances, or giving something of value to others so that they will become *recommenders* of the Millennial Hotels online community.

Stage One: Creating the Millennials Online Community

My first step is to create an online community, ported to mobile phones as well, called www.MillennialHotels.com. The community will enable its users to have a joyful experience in seeing floor plans and other amenities of every Millennial Hotels property in every city, along with rates and deals. The community site will be a multipage portal, with very few words and lots of art and design. The viewer will not be carpet bombed with ads on any of the pages. The visitor will not be hit with a subscription fee. The visitor will not be terrorized with requests to reveal a lot of demographic information, because in so doing Millennial Hotels would be perceived as untrustworthy. The first step is to make a friend of the visitor and to build his trust in the community.

The visitor presumably is taking a trip and needs a hotel. The Millennial Hotels community will take a little longer to book the reservation, but there will be so much fun and design involved that the trade-off will be worth the extra 10 or 15 minutes.

On the first page of the Millennial Hotels community portal, the potential occupant will see the floor plan of the target property, the exercise room, sauna, swimming pool, lounge, restaurants, jog path and the room sizes and shapes to choose from. This page will be laid out in brilliant graphics, with warm colors mixed with edgy shapes. The occupant can select her room, based on the floor plans, put up her credit card to reserve the room, and then the fun begins!

First, the occupant turns to the next page on the portal, where she will be able to design her room with an inventory of lighting, furniture, art, linens and bathroom accessories provided by Millennial Hotels' inventory room, the second page in the community portal. The occupant can lay out the room to her liking. Then it gets better. She can select the music that she wants to hear when she enters the room for the first time and thereafter. She does this by going to the next page on the portal, where she sees four turntables; she clicks on each to put together a montage of the sounds she loves—some Ella Fitzgerald, the theme from *Elvira Madigan* (Mozart Piano Concerto No. 21), Norah Jones, and Ray Charles and Friends, for instance.

Then she turns to the fourth page on the portal and selects the wine that she would like to have delivered to her room to await her arrival. She is generating the way she wants to be treated at the hotel. She can indicate the temperature of the wine—some reds should be served cooler than others, for instance.

The next page on the community portal will be called the sharing pages. Here the occupant will enter her designed and accessorized room into a "kudos contest." (See www.CokeMusic.com for a similar social network.) The occupant can enter her room into a contest with rooms designed by other soon-to-be occupants of the same property. When a visitor to the kudos contest likes the room designs he sees, the visitor can give kudos to that designer. Remember, everyone is pseudonymous, so the gender, age and profile of the kudo giver is unknown to the kudo receiver. There is mystery and fun in the psuedonymity, as you will see later.

The kudos can be valued at three different denominations, say $5, $10 and $20. Occupant number five can give a $20 kudo to occupant number 17, which could be a way of saying, "I'll be staying at the Millennial Hotel in Denver when you're there, and I hope to meet you."

The recipient of the kudos will collect these chits much as she would collect frequent stayer points, to be used in the Millennial Hotels chain; to be used to purchase drinks in the Denver Millennial Hotel lounge when she stays there in a week; or to be traded on IGE for cash, just as one trades Palladium Dust earned in the mythical land of Norrath in EverQuest II.

For reservations made on the fly, the community will be ported to mobile phones. The carriers—Verizon, AT&T, Spring and T-Mobile in the United States, with Orange, Three, Vodaphone and others in Europe—will enjoy the extra revenue from connect time or from showing off one's room design to a friend who hasn't yet joined the Millennial Hotels community. That's a 10 cent charge to the receiver's mobile phone. The carriers generally keep 35 cents on the dollar earned from their licensing deals with mobile social networks, and pay the content creator 65 cents every month for the prior month's minute usage on their network. This revenue channel to Millennial Hotels could become very significant because business travelers often book their reservations on the fly, while taking a taxi to the airport, or when their airplane is sitting on the tarmac waiting to take off. ShopQwik.com, a UK start-up, offers a mobil-based room reservations service. The new revenue channel for the carriers means that they will support the Millennial Hotels community with ads on their web sites and in off-line ads.

Finding the First Customers

To kick off the Millennial Hotels community, I would use virtual marketing tools. I would persuade bloggers known for their ability to influence people and to persuade opinion makers to view the community portal in beta and to make a hypothetical reservation, do a room design, select music, order wine and join the kudos contest. Then I would have these well-known bloggers write about their experiences, with Millennials paying a $1,000 reward or giving five free nights to the author of the best story. Then I would see that the stories were massively blogged to the print and online media. I would work virtual marketing aggressively, by planting decoy Millennial Hotels lovers on Facebook, LinkedIn and other communities where people can be persuaded more easily by a "friend."

I would seek strategic partners among the online travel search companies, such as Travelocity and Expedia, and swap packages with them—one hundred discounted rooms for them to sell in exchange for their putting a Millennial Hotels community link on their home page.

I would use good old-fashioned multilevel marketing techniques with early adopters, awarding them one free night for every 55 visitors they send to the Millennial Hotels community portal. I would seek publicity only in online newsletters, not in print or TV media, because old media is not trusted by the millennials the way new media is.

On the fifth page of the portal I would offer a storytelling contest. Occupants would be encouraged to write about their experiences in making a reservation and designing a room and about how they met an old high school friend or someone whom they eventually married at the kudos contest page. Millennial Hotels can ask for stories to be written and posted every month, with all members of the community encouraged to vote for the best stories on the topic of "My Millennials Experience in June 2007." Only members of the community can vote. The winner will be awarded something of value by Millennial Hotels, such as 500 kudo points, or five free nights at Millennial Hotel's Hawaii resort.

Subliminal Marketing

Pseudonymous meetings in the kudos contest could lead to potential occupants of the same hotel asking one another via e-mail, "When are you going to be at the Denver Millennial?" The respondent might answer, "Next week. When will you be there?" And the curious occupant might answer, "Same time. Say, I really liked your room and your music selection. I wonder if we could meet for dinner or . . ." If the appropriate atmosphere is created, people may come to Millennial Hotels' community in order to actually meet people for social or romantic reasons, at a particular Millennial property. It is said by some that the virtual community SecondLife is used by graying gamers to meet fellow players in real life for social or romantic reasons.

Events, experiences, games, storytelling, design and fun—all are user-generated. This will create the most unique travel experience in the hospitality industry.

17

Medical Research

ONE OF THE REASONS that the U.S. Defense Department conceived of the need for ARPANET (the progenitor of the Internet) in 1986, and based it at a handful of research-oriented universities such as Cornell and Stanford, was to enable cutting-edge medical information to move seamlessly from the locus of the knowledge to the point where it was urgently needed. That need still exists, notwithstanding that certain Web portals such as Eurekah.com contain the most advanced medical research and sell it on a relatively inexpensive subscription basis.

People who are affected with life-threatening diseases, such as Lou Gehrig's disease, have joined together in chat rooms for a decade. The same applies to diabetes and breast cancer victims. But these chat rooms give more in the way of encouragement than Web logs provided by researchers whose latest work could provide life-saving therapies to the chatters.

The entrepreneurial solution is simple, but so many of the great ones are. An entrepreneur forms a new company, let's call it TheraPeep, Inc.—a combination of *therapy* and the sound of a happy bird, "peep," which all sick people want to be sure they are listening to in 10 years. TheraPeep creates a Web portal called www.TheraPeep.com where it advertises "cutting-edge medical therapies for every disease" for $20 per year. With its initial capital plus the $20 subscription fees, TheraPeep licenses the cutting-edge research published in Science, the *New England Journal of Medicine*, the *Journal of the American Medical Association*, Lancet, Eurekah .com and elsewhere and makes it available to its subscribers. The subscribers then may share the information with nonsubscribers, but a digital rights manager (DRM) prevents the free use of the information by a nonsubscriber, who then pays her $20/year to TheraPeep.com or does not, as she wishes.

The people with diseases who join TheraPeep.com will, in many cases, know more about possible therapies than will their physicians. By sharing data with their fellow sufferers, their knowledge will grow cumulatively, and the groups' knowledge will become the wisdom of crowds, as described by James Surowiecki:

> The idea of the wisdom of crowds also takes decentralization as a given and a good, since it implies that if you set a crowd of self-interested, independent people to work in a decentralized way on the same problem, instead of trying to direct their efforts from the top down, their collective solution is likely to be better than any other solution you could come up with.
>
> —James Surowiecki, *The Wisdom of Crowds*

Holding the TheraPeep business model up to the $P \times S \times E$ equation produces a huge valuation for both P and S, because there are so many life-threatening diseases and there are many cutting-edge therapies that need to be discussed by the mobs to enable their wisdom to apply. The E factor is not causal, but rather determined by the founders of TheraPeep. They can choose business partners who do things well, to use the Drucker aphorism, or they can choose friends who have a few bucks in their pocket, or were once physicians (who do not make good businesspeople as a general rule.)

The DEJ factors affecting TheraPeep are all positive as well. People with life-threatening diseases are many, have a relatively standard need and will pay for a solution—discussion of new, cutting-edge therapies to save their lives. There is no barrier to entry, in fact the Constitution encourages free speech, notwithstanding that the pharmaceutical companies might enter the TheraPeep community for the purpose of making claims about their palliatives, and these defectors will have to be rooted out.

The "Float Many Clubs" test works as well. This is a definitely a community that can charge a subscription fee—the scarce resource factor applies—and not offend anyone. There can be a fund set aside for potential members who cannot afford $1.66 a month, and on the home page it can be stated that $1.00 out of every $20.00 in annual dues will be set aside to enable those who cannot afford membership to be admitted with payment from others. For those who cannot afford a computer and an Internet connection, TheraPeep should quietly pay for them, including set-up and training, in cooperation with the nearest ISP. A not-for-profit subsidiary of TheraPeep can solicit donations for these people and participate as well with 10 percent of its net profits.

The "Many" factor has a positive value as well. Members should be grouped with members who share their affliction in order to maximize the value of the exchange of knowledge. There are more than 2 million women in the United States living with breast cancer and they want to have a conversation with others who have breast cancer, and not with migraine headache sufferers. Storytelling will be very positive for all of the members. There is value in telling one's life story to friends, and possibly similarities among the members of the breast cancer group as to their mother's health, their grandmother's health, stressors that they encountered in life, their children and their happiness in life in general. WeightWatchers International's success is based on people paying for the right to engage in storytelling, so that's your precedent.

The "Clubs" factor is questionable. There may not be any value whatsoever in the afflicted people flying to a convention center somewhere to meet. It may not strengthen their bonds of trust developed pseudonymously and in fact might weaken them. People speak more freely if they can hide behind an IP address. To "come out into the open" and face their favorite co-sufferers in person could have a negative effect.

Absent this last factor, and giving the E factor a 2 rather than a 3 rating, I calculate a score of 39 for TheraPeep, and I encourage you communiteers who have followed this far into the book to consider this smart start-up. You will need a few bucks up front to visit the sources of cutting-edge, breakthrough, life-saving therapies, and this could mean buying data from Eurekah.com and the magazines *Science*, *JAMA*, *Nature* and so forth. It will be necessary for you to assemble a board of wise people from the medical profession to help keep the truth in and the placeboes out. Licensing DRM software to block the sending of information to a non-member will be important, and an important means of finding new members. And TheraPeep will require some staunch marketing up front, including blog marketing and search engine optimization (SEO), which is pricey when the subject is health and medicine. This launch could cost around $1.5 million.

As a general rule, the higher the score in smart start-ups business model scoring systems, the less the amount of launch capital needed.

18

Life Insurance

THE MODEL FOR a life insurance community is so embarrassingly simple that I have to think it's out there in this new ecosystem of communities; but if it isn't, I will contribute a thought or two. Men and women with families, and perhaps grandchildren, now have a means of leaving behind for these younger generations a pictorial, video and textual life story. They are able to do so because you are going to create a community for them; let's call it www.OldFolksLifeStories.com.

OldFolks, for short, will seek out people who want their children, grandchildren and great-grandchildren to understand what it was like for them to grow up, achieve certain things, fail at others, find their perfect life partner, raise children and take memorable vacations, make lasting friends, build an important collection for their descendants to enjoy and so forth. The community follows Daniel Pink's axiom that storytelling is the highest form of communication, and storytelling will be one of the stars of the age of communities.

This community is certainly worth charging a subscription for, because it is a form of vanity publishing, and vanity publishers charge for printing and binding books that cannot find mainline publishers.

But there are myriad other revenue channels in the OldFolks business model. Many people of a certain age can send e-mails and type Word documents, but they'll be darned if they know how to insert a photo, much less a video. The OldFolks community owners can provide assistance to its members in putting in the pictures and the videos, even using PowerPoint from time to time to make a powerful point.

A typical subscription fee might be $60 a year, to maintain the person's historical record and to permit updates annually or more frequently. The service fee to add pictures and videos and to provide background music could range from $100 to $5,000, depending on the desired features.

Let's say Jim Smith wants to describe the long and beautiful courtship that he enjoyed with his wife of 45 years, Mary Daniels Smith. He writes eloquently and lovingly of how they were introduced at the wedding of a mutual friend, but didn't see each other for several months, as both went off to college. Then they happened to bump into each other in the American Airlines terminal in Indianapolis airport, when both were held over due to rain. They were flying to Chicago. Jim suggested that he rent a car and they could drive. He would drop her at her home, then go to his family's home and turn in the car the next day. Mary was okay with that. Jim and Mary hopped into the Ford, and they chatted most of the way, until Jim thought he noticed Mary drooping her head as if to sleep. To stay awake, he turned on the radio softly to a rock 'n' roll station, and the Dixie Cups were singing the number one song of 1964, "Chapel of Love":

> Spring is here
> The sky is blue
> Whoa, Whoa, Whoa
> Birds all sing
> As if they knew
> Today's the day
> We'll say I do
> And we'll never be lonely anymore
>
> Because we're going to the chapel
> And we're gonna get married
> Yes, we're going to the chapel
> And we're gonna get ma-a-arried

Jim wants his grandchildren in particular to hear this song, and he needs to know if he can download the soundtrack into his historical record, or is it copyrighted and must he pay a royalty? And if he can download it, with or without a royalty payment, would the technical people at OldFolks help him do it? Sure, for a charge.

It turns out that there is great significance to "Chapel of Love." It seems that Mary wasn't sleeping at all, but rather feigning sleep, with her eyes slightly open to see what Jim was like when he was alone. Did he talk to himself, hum ditties, remove his false eye, pick his ears with a pencil? She was getting to like him, and she wanted to watch him when he thought he wasn't being watched. She learned one thing: He surely liked "Chapel of Love."

Their courtship continued for several months, and finally they were almost constantly in one another's company because Mary transferred to Miami University where Jim was. Jim seemed nervous about settling down with one girl, when there were so many beauties out there. He also had a high draft number for the Vietnam War, and didn't want to marry Mary and then leave her for Saigon. So on a spring evening, like the one in Indianapolis, the two of them were making out and Mary, who had preset the turntable with a 45 loaded onto the spindle, hit a button with her free hand and the Dixie Cups began singing, "Spring is here, the sky is blue. Whoa, Whoa, Whoa." And Jim looked at her, and asked, amazed and amused, "You weren't asleep on the drive to Chicago?"

"No, I watched you enjoying this song."

"Do you like the song, Mary?" Jim asked.

"I think I like it as much as you do," she replied.

"Then I would like to go to the chapel with you, Mary. Will you marry me?"

And Mary answered, along with the Dixie Cups, "I'll say I do, and we'll never be lonely anymore."

That memory pretty much has to have pictures of the wedding and "Chapel of Love" as background music.

The OldFolks owners could add a $150 service charge for incorporating pictures and the song. Jim would be so heartened by the vividness it lent to his story, that he might ask for the OldFolks team to assist him with videos and music for other memorable events, such as the birth of his and Mary's children, their first real home and their first trip to Hawaii.

The Mathematics

If OldFolks signs up 20,000 members in the first year for $30 apiece and if each member needs $300 in services, they will achieve first-year revenues of $6.6 million. With so much of the content generated by members, the gross profit margin will be around $6 million. Assuming a staff of 20 to assist the members with their uploads and music, with each employee earning $70,000 plus benefits of another $30,000 a year, those costs would come to $2 million, leaving OldFolks with net operating income of $4 million before corporate overhead. The revenue growth could come from word of mouth, viral marketing, SEO and e-mail marketing to a list of names rented from AARP.

OldFolks could also be an interesting joint venture with an insurance carrier such as Metropolitan Life or John Hancock. The goodwill they could build with this community could be immense, if they tiptoe around it and avoid firing popup ads into beautiful stories like that of Jim and Mary.

But in exchange for providing the start-up capital to the founders of OldFolks, and taking a small ownership position, Metropolitan Life could be given the right to award "unexpected bonuses" to the authors of the most inspiring stories. The contest doesn't have to be announced, and shouldn't be announced, because nothing builds loyalty to a brand like unexpected rewards and bonuses. With the winning authors' permission, the top stories could be published in Metropolitan Life's annual report.

The insurance company sponsor of OldFolks could also contribute names of people who might want to store their life stories in an online community vault, thus lowering OldFolks' cost of finding the first customers.

If the community grows to 2 million members, each of whom pays $50 a year and 20 percent of whom pay for services worth $500 a year, this amazing revenue machine grosses $1.2 billion a year and earns about $1.1 billion. If the OldFolks founders took it public, it would capture a market value (using Yahoo's market-to-revenue ratio of 20×) of $24 billion. If acquired by a life insurance company (and relatively few are large enough to acquire it) as a new business feeder and contributor to earnings, the life insurance company would probably begin trading like a hot community stock.

Could OldFolks reshape the way life insurance is sold? Could storytelling by the user provide just the right setting for the user to be offered an insurance policy? Could life insurance companies be permitted to post some soft-sell banners, along with resort communities, cruises and boats, on the OldFolks' home page? These are ideas worth considering.

19

Replacing Advertising with Reputation Management

YOU ARE STANDING in front of the cough medicine shelf at Walgreen's because you have a terrible cough. You haven't watched television or read a newspaper or national magazine in years. You have not had a cough in years. You don't know NyQuil from Robitussin, Vicks, Sudafed or Walgreen's private label product. But that doesn't matter. Consumer product advertising has been downsized because it has been replaced with reputation management. Here's how it works.

There is a radio frequency identification (RFID) chip attached to each box of cough syrup. Imbedded in the RFID chip are opinions about each product, provided by real consumers of the products. Each consumer provides an oral description of his or her cough, what it felt like, if it was dry or phlegmy, and if it produced a fever, runny nose, red eyes, fatigue and so forth. Then they describe why DayQuil worked or why Robitussin did the trick. Perhaps they took the cough syrup with an herbal remedy, such as echinacea or osha root.

You retrieve and listen to these oral comments by dialing into reputation manager.net on your cell phone. You listen to the cough-beating remedies of real people like yourself and make the appropriate purchase.

Near Field Communication

Near Field Communication (NFC) is a wireless connectivity technology that enables short-range communications between electronic devices, such as RFID tags and mobile phones. Simply by bringing two NFC-enabled devices close together, they automatically initiate network communications without requiring the user to configure the setup. It has the power to replace the credit card, because an NFC-enabled mobile phone and a ticket or invoice-issuing device can interact at an airport ticketing machine, an ATM, a grocery store or a computer. In the hypothetical drugstore or supermarket that we have been discussing, an NFC-enabled mobile phone can read the URL from a smart label, or an RFID tag, and thereby identify the product and ascertain the price.

By Invitation Only

Now, let's return to our community, which we will call ManyPeoples Choice.com. For this community, which will appeal mostly to adults, people with money and people concerned about using their money efficiently, I am going to borrow a business model made famous by American Express: by invitation only. Not just anyone can join ManyPeoplesChoice.com.

It's much too exclusive to permit the riffraff to join. After all, it costs $10 a month to be a member. By making this community gated, it will be relatively easy to offer an affinity card, just like American Express does, and follow that with a catalogue of approved products—approved by the community, of course.

I would take this community upscale and capture the high ground. It would have a board of directors with unimpeachable credentials, a board of advisers from the medical and nutrition communities and an esteemed educator. This is a board to ask Colin Powell and Dr. Robert Jarvik, the inventor of the artificial heart, to join.

The first online community to be by invitation only was Mixi, founded by 30-year-old Kenji Kasahara, who cut his teeth in entrepreneurship with FindJob.com in 1997. That didn't work out, because he could find companies seeking people, but he couldn't find people to fill the positions. It dawned on him that social networking was the way to attract people, and in 2004, Kasahara founded Mixi in Japan. He decided to make it special—as the American Express slogan goes, "Membership has its privileges."

At Mixi the members know each other; they are not as pseudonymous or as anonymous as in most communities. They have come to Mixi for the same reasons: to find wonderful jobs. They help each other. They recommend employers to each other. In 18 months, Mixi has attracted 5 million members who pay subscription fees. The community receives 10 million unique visits a day.

Kasahara took Mixi public on September 14, 2006, and became an instant paper billionaire with 64 percent of Mixi's stock.

The Cost of Launching ManyPeoplesChoice.com

The manufacturers of NFC devices—Nokia, Philips and Sony—formed the NFC Forum last year. Subsequently MasterCard, Matsushita, Microsoft, Motorola, Samsung, Texas Instruments and Visa joined. They were followed by American Express, LG, Intel, Siemens and Sony Ericsson. Presumably they are at a point in product development at which they are beta-testing and setting standards for the NFC device.

Soon there will be a product and a price, and when that occurs, this community can be a first customer. How much will the devices cost? Will they be $150 or $1,500? Planning for the higher end of the price spectrum makes sense. Budgeting 1,000 devices at $600 apiece, or $600,000, makes sense. Distributing 200 to early-bird signers for free also seems sensible. The early birds can be encouraged to invite friends to join for a commission, ala Mary Kay parties; and the "privilege" they will receive for joining will be a discounted price for a first-generation NFC device.

Encouraging drugstore and supermarket chains will burn through quite a lot of working capital. They have to see the advantage. The advantage is eventual, far into the future: lower prices to them because their vendors will spend less on advertising. It's a tough sell, but others who have sold point-of-sale products (mini billboards on supermarket shopping carts from Act Media comes to mind) bore the heavy marketing cost. Budget $500,000 for this.

Then there are the systems engineers, the servers, the intense programming of transmitters and receivers, which could run another million dollars before breakeven is reached.

Measuring Breakeven

To calculate breakeven, you divide annualized fixed costs into one over gross profit margin. If the devices are sold to members for $750 apiece, and there are 1,000 first-year members who, in addition, pay $100 a year in dues, then the cost of goods sold margin is $600/850, or 70 percent. If you then divide 0.70 by $1.5 million (fixed operating costs), you get $4.6 million as the annual revenue level needed to break even. Add 20 percent to this figure for unexpected delays and exogenous variables to arrive at $5.52 million, and you see that ManyPeoplesChoice.com will need close to 7,000 members to reach breakeven.

As that might not occur for two years, the community will need to cover another year of operating costs, or $1.5 million, plus another $1 million in working capital reserve to support device lease-purchase financing, or $2.5 million total. Add that to the first year's start-up costs of $2.1 million and the total budget comes to $4.6 million.

With a large enough lever, a person could move the earth. With $4.6 million, a communiteer could forever change how consumer goods and services are marketed. That is a staggering thought, and one of you will probably do it.

Community for Ardent Fans
of College Sports

OVER THE PAST SEVERAL YEARS, rotisserie sports pools, known as fantasy sports leagues, have expanded from the office and bar environments to the Internet. Every major Internet portal—ESPN.com, SI.com and Yahoo .com—actively maintains some of the most robust rotisserie leagues on the Web, while Head2Head.com has built its entire business model around rotisserie football, baseball, basketball, racing, golf and hockey. They focus entirely on rotisserie leagues and rotisserie pools for Division 1 football and basketball.

Let's give this new company a name: Thorpe.com, in honor of Jim Thorpe. The rotisserie leagues on Thorpe.com can model themselves on the Head2Head sports revenue concept, but with a Division 1 college football and basketball focus. The users will be known as "general managers." They can choose to participate in leagues focusing exclusively on the Southeastern Conference (SEC), Atlantic Coast Conference (ACC), Big 10, Big 12, or PAC 10, or they can participate in leagues that allow rosters to be drawn from all Division 1 sports programs.

There are many possible revenue streams derivable from fantasy leagues. These include initial team registrations as well as trades that general managers purchase during the course of a season to replace injured or underperforming players. These revenues will allow Thorpe.com the ability to provide prizes to general managers for weekly performances, and for overall performance in respective leagues.

Features of Thorpe.com

Let's explore some of the revenue-generating features possible in this college sports community

NCAA Basketball Tournament

The NCAA Basketball tournament is one of the most watched sporting events in the world. In 2006, ESPN gave out a $10,000 grand prize for the winner of their NCAA basketball tournament. Amazingly, of their 3 million entrants, only four individuals correctly guessed the Final Four combination. This sporting event is important to any site in the fact that it drives viewers to sites every day for the three-week period known as "March Madness." The owners of Thorpe.com will be able to compete with ESPN by creating their own free bracket platform as a tool to drive users to the other Division 1 sports fantasy games.

Insider News Content

ESPN, *Sports Illustrated* and every major professional sports team (plus local newspapers) sell special "insider" sports news and comments on an annual subscription fee basis. These fees are not excessive and range from $10 to $100 for an annual subscription. Much of the raw data and news feeds that Thorpe.com collects as part of the daily business can be included in these insider pages.

This information is as simple as pregame and post-game interviews with players, coaches and athletic directors; injury reports; statistics; predictions; high school signings; focus pages on coaches and players (who they are and what they like to do in their spare time); coaching tips (for Pop Warner coaches and high school coaches); comprehensive schedules; historical records of each team and video replays of significant plays during the season.

Internet Streaming of Existing Broadcasts

The company's existing broadcasts are free (although advertising supported) via the radio stations in the network, but many potential customers are outside of broadcast footprints or are unable to listen to programs at the time of broadcast. The company plans on streaming the broadcast through the web site and allowing listeners to enjoy existing broadcast content for free or for a small fee.

Collegiate Apparel Sales

By clicking right through the existing web site, visitors will be able to access college bookstores of every Division 1 university with a link on the site.

Revenue can be derived two ways from this: first, by tracking payments through the company's payment portal at a university bookstore page and receiving a percentage of each sale; and second, by obtaining a reseller agreement from the major clothing companies that produce collegiate apparel and selling their products directly through the company site. Either way, collegiate apparel sales are a big business that generates significant revenues, and Thorpe.com can position itself to capture a small portion of these revenues.

Ticket Brokering

Purchasing tickets online is a large part of all events, not just sporting events. Ticketmaster.com and eBay give people the opportunity to purchase tickets to all events, throughout the country. It is perfectly legal (but certain laws do apply regarding ticket pricing). There are many Internet sites that are dedicated to brokering tickets for sporting events, concerts, and so on. Thorpe.com will be ideally positioned to get a foothold in college sporting events by focusing on Division 1 sports alone.

Radio Tie-in

Thorpe.com can bring a new dimension to community: a call-in radio talk show that is conference specific. With cash flow from its other businesses, Thorpe.com will develop a radio program that provides comprehensive coverage of the major NCAA Division 1 Conferences, broadcasting Monday through Friday, from 5:00 to 8:00 P.M. local time, from its headquarters city. The program can be made available via satellite throughout the United States. The broadcasts will be advertising-supported.

The radio programs will be hosted by teams of well-known, top-notch professional hosts and consummate on-air broadcast professionals. All of the radio hosts will necessarily have developed personal and working relationships with each of the specific region's coaches, athletic directors, university and conference officials.

Advertisers and the Pipeline of Potential Advertisers

The market that Thorpe.com seeks to capture is perhaps the most sought-after consumer market in the country: the upwardly mobile, college-educated young male market. Each person in this market is automatically a member of an affinity group. He is an alumnus of a school that plays Division 1 athletics. If it is the SEC, Big 12 or PAC 10, the affinity group is primarily college football. If it is the ACC, Big East or Big 10, it is primarily college basketball.

Advertisers of beverages, automobiles, trucks, sporting goods, travel and apparel would give their eyeteeth to capture the attention of this market. Thorpe.com will necessarily want to design affinity-based marketing pieces for its advertisers to enable them to offer college-specific products sponsored by such-and-such advertiser. What alumnus of Notre Dame wouldn't like to have an overhead photograph of the football stadium, sponsored by Budweiser or Travelocity? What alumnus of Duke University wouldn't like a signed photograph of Coach "K" sponsored by Chevrolet? It does not require a brain surgeon to develop a successful advertising and sponsorship program.

However, advertisers, particularly the major national brands, want to see a national rollout of the broadcast network before committing advertising dollars. They have witnessed plans for new media rollouts in the past, some of which made it, such as ads on supermarket shopping carts, and some of which did not—like coupons that pop out of shelves as consumers walk by. National advertisers are cautious.

Market Facts

Thorpe.com will be targeting the leaders in innovation from almost 2,000 radio stations, which comprise the broadcast networks of the NCAA Division 1 schools, and whose listener audience is primarily the male population, ages 25 to 54, nationally. By 2010, this segment of the population is projected by demographers to number more than 60 million (projected from 2000 Census Data, Database: C90STF1A, at www.census .gov). Given the demographic trends of the past two decades, this increase since the 1990s will almost assuredly continue well into the next several decades.

Collegiate sports fans display the following outstanding (for advertisers) demographic qualitative profile:

- Over 60 percent hold professional/managerial positions.
- Over 90 percent are college graduates.
- Over 60 percent have attended graduate school.
- Over 67 percent own corporate stock.
- Over 61 percent have annual median household income over $55,000.
- Over 22 percent have annual median household income over $150,000.
- Over 70 percent travel by air.

- Approximately 52 percent reside in the city where their favored university is located.
- Over 65 percent reside in the state where their favored university is located.

(*Source:* Collegiate Sports Publishing, Field Research Corporation.)

Strategic Alliances and Partnerships

Thorpe.com has a wide berth to select from in choosing the most desirable strategic partners. A national broadcasting network and/or chain of radio stations would be a perfect fit. A sports agnostic shoe, cap or apparel maker such as Nike would be an outstanding partner as well. A beer, potato chip, peanut or hot dog producer, or all four, could be given most favored national advertising positions, in exchange for making a strategic alliance investment up front that would pay for some of the start-up costs.

21

A Community of Art Dealers

HOW WOULD YOU LIKE to browse paintings and sculptures for your home or office from a visual database of substantially all art and sculpture available through galleries at the moment you are buying? It is technologically possible through an online community of art dealers.

A community of art dealers and art gallery owners displaying on virtual walls the art they have contracted to sell, as well as the art of other dealers and gallery owners, is definitely an idea whose time has come because it adds enormously to the liquidity of the art market. The business model would work like this. First of all, art dealers and gallery owners would agree to join a community for $5,000 a year. Let's say that 1,000 of them sign up; you've just raised $5 million in working capital without selling a share of stock. Let's call the community www.ShareOurArt.com.

With their money, you build a strong search engine and broadband distribution capability that enables the galleries and dealers to share the work of different artists. Let's say Mary Smith is looking for a black-and-white drawing of a horse, measuring about three feet by four feet, by artist Joseph Piccillo. Mary goes to her nearest art gallery, Jones Art, and asks him for a Piccillo horse with those specifications. Mr. Jones, who doesn't carry Piccillo but is a member of the ShareOurArt.com community, dials in and asks who represents Piccillo, and finds that is a gallery in New York City by the name of York Fine Art. York Fine Art's inventory of Piccillo is quickly uploaded to Mr. Jones' PC and he sees several black and white horses. Mr. Jones displays the Piccillo drawings for his client, Mary Smith, on his wall, using a projector attached to his computer, and she buys the piece she wants. Under the terms of the ShareOurArt.com revenue-sharing agreement, Mr. Jones pays York Fine Art 35 percent and he keeps 15 percent of the selling price. York Fine Arts pays the artist 50 percent.

The community that you run enables art gallery owners and dealers to dramatically increase their revenues, because now they represent *all* artists, not just a handful. Furthermore, they do not have to hang the original pieces of art on their walls; they can display the work at full size and with precise colors by projecting them onto the wall from the computer. The gallery owners save on wall space rental and inventory handling costs.

Thousands of artists who are unable to obtain gallery representation could sign up with ShareOurArt.com as well by paying you a representation fee—and if they cannot afford a fee, by giving up a number of pieces for free. A division of ShareOurArt.com—let's call it the "bullpen"—will digitally photograph the art of the unrepresented artists and make their work available to galleries and customers who are seeking art by unspecified artists. Frequently, consumers of art seek a certain size, shape, color and theme to go above a couch or a buffet. Above all, they want the right width and height, the right color combination and a soft or edgy theme. The bullpen section of ShareOurArt.com could be a good fit for their desires and their budget.

ShareOurArt.com solves several problems—the P factor—by pumping more liquidity and inventory into the marketplace. Art galleries have a limited amount of wall space. Because they are situated on highly trafficked streets, their wall space is costly. Thus, they charge artists from 40 to 60 percent of the retail price of a painting in exchange for hanging their works of art. With ShareOurArt.com, gallery owners add to their wall space the wall space of every other gallery owner who joins the online community.

The pressure to join the community will be applied by the artists. Because they will surely sell more of their work if their universe of possible buyers is expanded infinitely, the artists will attempt to get out of their contracts with gallery owners who gainsay ShareOurArt.com in order to sign on with gallery owners who are active members.

Responsibilities of the Owner of ShareOurArt.com

Gallery owners are not the silent, withdrawn types. You will have your hands full keeping them content. Thus, I recommend charging them up front and asking for a fairly hefty membership fee—$5,000 for the year sounds about right. You can take a lot of getting your butt chewed if the butt-chewer pays you enough.

There will be complaints about technology; so it's best that you unify the technology, so that every gallery owner leases or buys from you a server and a projector that is identical to every other member's equipment. Then you can overnight or swap out replacement equipment if needed.

You will need to be the record keeper and the transaction observer to assure your members that each of them is being treated fairly. ShareOur Art.com would have to know the retail price of every painting and every sculpture in the system at all times. By knowing all inventory, prices and transactions, ShareOurArt.com will know if the art gallery that "lent" the inventory to the art gallery that sold the inventory received a fair deal. An artist may receive a check for $10,000 and have, say, a 60/40 arrangement with her dealer. She can dial into a password-protected page in ShareOurArt.com Web portal and see that one of her pieces recently sold for $16,670. The assurance will bind her to ShareOurArt.com like white binds to rice.

ShareOurArt.com will shine light into a marketplace that has been opaque for years. Some artists have been taken to the cleaners by their dealers. Their checks have been held up for months. Their checks have borne incorrect amounts. Their work has been off the walls for months at a time. But with ShareOurArt.com, artists will sell much more art and they will receive their checks without hassle.

Everyone benefits in this model, and if it is ported to mobile phones, the owners of ShareOurArt.com can gain another revenue channel. Offering an e-wallet, branded form of payment to this community, and a quarterly hardbound and online fee-based price list—to be sold to customers of the galleries to enable them to see the value of their investments rise or fall—brings several more revenue channels to the founders of ShareOurArt.com.

22

A Group Travel Community

IT'S 1662. Virgil and his friend Silas have built their log cabins in Schenectady, New York, and their wives are busy sewing and gardening. Silas says, "Virgil, let's hunt us some bear."

Virgil responds, "Silas, there are only two of us, and it would be unsafe for only two men to hunt a bear."

"You're right," Silas answers. " I wonder if there are some fellows in Poughkeepsie who might be interested in joining us."

"Let's send Luke down to Poughkeepsie to find us two more bear hunters. He makes the trip with his apples to sell at the Hudson River dock once a week."

"Good idea," Silas says.

That was then. Nowadays, when Silas and Virgil want to play golf, let's say, or hunt elk in Canada, they will go to a group travel community started by you, a reader of this book. Each will pay $150 a year for membership, and the services you provide in the community are pairing up golfers, helicopter skiers, fox hunters, quail hunters and so forth who want to take expensive and luxurious group sporting trips but lack enough friends to go with. Let's call the community PairingUp.com.

Silas and Virgil in 2006 want to play golf at St. Andrews and they specify the kinds of people they'd like to form a group with. They find a good offering on PairingUp.com. Off-line group travel organizations are welcome to join your community if they pay an advertising fee to your site based on cost per thousand (CPM), and that's a second source of revenue to your company.

Silas and Virgil say they would like 18 other members of the community to join them in order to get the discounted group rate. They would prefer men between 30 and 40 whose handicaps are under 15 and who in addition like good conversation and perhaps some poker in the evenings. Quickly, members of the community begin pumping e-mails at Silas's and Virgil's computers, and a compatible group of 20 golfers is put together on your community site. Each golfer pays your community $150, your third source of revenues.

Of course there will be a need for a reputation management software to prevent an insurance salesman or personal injury lawyer, or equivalent, from joining the group and trolling for new business from the first tee at Casa de Campo.

Business Model

I see three large revenue sources in this community. The first is people who seek other people, folks whom they might enjoy spending a week or 10 days with on the golf courses of Scotland, or on Safari in Kenya or deep sea fishing near the Galapagos. The second comes from group travel for golfers, hunters, fishermen and women and ecotourists among others; and the third is the fee paid upon assembling the right group for the right trip.

Assuming a membership price of $150 per year for the group travel seekers and $1,500 a year for the group travel providers, plus a $150 per person fee when the first group pays the group travel arrangers, first-year revenues might look something like those listed in Table 22.1. If 5,000 men and women sign up, you've got $750,000 in working capital to design and build out the site.

This community is not a particularly costly operation. For years and years, people like Virgil and Silas have flown off to play golf in Scotland or search for the white rhino in the Amboseli on the Kenya-Tanzania border. But when they arrived, their playing or safari partners were much

TABLE 22.1   First-Year Revenues for PairingUp.com

Type of Participant	Number of Participants	Fee	Total Revenues
Group travel seekers	10,000	$150.00 annual membership fee	$1,500,000
Group travel planners	500	$1,500.00 annual membership fee	$ 750,000
Group traveler members who buy a trip in the first year	3,000	$150.00 trip closing fee	$ 450,000
Estimated first year revenues			$2,700,000

older, too liberal, too loud, too abstemious of liquor and ale or just plain old pains in the asses. PairingUp.com will eliminate the risk of meeting up with the wrong people, by using questionnaires and psychological tests and screening methods. Offering a 100 percent money-back guarantee if not completely satisfied is probably a good idea. Conversely, offering a $1,000 bonus to anyone who takes a PairingUp.com trip and writes the best story about it is another way to attract more customers—unexpected rewards represent member loyalty stokers.

Growth in Subsequent Years

The customer base of PairingUp.com is one of the most coveted in all of marketing—people who have money and who like to spend it. But, if you rent out the list or let advertisers in the door, you haven't read this book very well. Those are so wrong; so yesterday.

To grow this remarkable community, let the satisfied customers do their thing and let word-of-mouth viral marketing by using the best bloggers do its thing. Keep a low profile and avoid the media, because your model can be copied easily. Get the users involved with storytelling and an affinity e-wallet card. Encourage more than one trip a year.

23

Partnering with Giant Corporations

HUNDREDS, PERHAPS THOUSANDS of large consumer products and service companies will catch wind of the communiteering buzz and seek to hire a communiteer to develop and operate a corporation-sponsored community. Because one of the underpinnings of an online community is truthfulness, you must be up front with the corporation that there will be no slackening of that rule in their community. Think of joint bidding with a proven software firm that builds online communities, such as OneSite.

To obtain communiteering jobs from large corporations, write to their business development offices, offering your services and explaining why they should nucleate their customers into online communities. Your guidebook may be this book, but go for it; quote me liberally and become a dues-paying member of Smartstartups.com.

A rereading of Chapter 1, particularly references to EDS, will be very useful to you, because you will be running a facilities management company. You will begin with just one client, but soon that number will grow to 20 or more. After all, Amazon.com runs the online storefronts for more than 50 retailers such as Barnes & Noble and Target, among others.

TABLE 23.1   Projected Third-Year Revenues

30 clients at $1 million/year each	$ 30,000,000
750,000 members × 30 clients × $10 per year in membership fees	225,000,000
22,500,000 newsletter subscriptions at $2.00/month	540,000,000
Total revenues	$795,000,000

Big corporations don't feel they are getting good service unless they are charged a lot of money. An annual fee of $1 million, paid one-twelfth in advance and monthly thereafter, seems like a reasonable price. The big corporations will be able to provide you with customer e-mail addresses from warranty cards and dealership records (in the case of automobiles). I don't think you will be able to charge a $20 membership fee, but you can test that pricing model, as well as a lower one. A newsletter for $2 per month may be an easier sell, because it will include juicy topics such as recommendations to improve the product.

I can give this business a score of 45 using the scoring system outlined in Chapter 6. It should be able to generate the revenues listed in Table 23.1 by year three with less than $6 million in annual expenditures for salaries, rent, web site design, hosting and marketing. I visualize 40 to 45 employees by the third year.

More than $750 million of those revenues should result in profit. This community-building and operating business should make its founders very wealthy indeed.

MyThirdPlace.com

THE AUTHORS of a thoroughly researched paper in the August 2006 edition of the *Journal of Computer-Mediated Communication* may have provided an idea for one of the greatest online communities: mythirdplace.com. Constance Steinkuehler and Dmitri Williams, professors in education and speech communication at the University of Wisconsin at Madison and the University of Illinois at Urbana-Champaign, respectively, claim that Morpegs and other online games promote sociability and new worldviews.

The games, the researchers write, act like virtual coffee shops and bars, places where "social bridging" takes place. They liken playing such games as Asheron's Call and Lineage to dropping in at Cheers, the fictional TV bar "where everybody knows your name."

And to put an even sharper point on it, Skeinkuehler and Williams argue that it is precisely the lack of real-world hangouts that "is driving the MMO phenomenon" in the first place. The title of their paper is fittingly "Where Everybody Knows Your (Screen) Name: Online Games as Third Places" (http://jcmc.indiana.edu/vol11/issue4/steinkuehler.html).

The phrase third place was coined by sociologist Ray Oldenburg in 1999 to describe the physical places outside the home and workplace that people use for informal social interaction. Steinkuehler and Williams propose that online games are third places that enable players, through their avatars, to interact with the gaming software and with other players, to build "relationships of status and solidarity." Williams takes the idea one leap forward. "In other words," he says, "spending time in these social games helps people meet others not like them, even if it doesn't always lead to strong friendships. That kind of social horizon-broadening has been sorely lacking in American society for decades."

Retribalization

To the keen eye of an entrepreneur trolling for the next MySpace or eBay, there is a big, big problem in need of a solution. The problem that Steinkuehler and Williams have identified is a hunger for third places by a great many people.

Neighborhoods have seen their downtown real-world hangouts closed and shuttered with the opening of big-box stores near interstate intersections. Getting together to play poker or mah-jongg in the evenings is more difficult with gasoline prices at $3.00 per gallon. Miniature golf, driving ranges, fun parks, movies followed by dinners out with friends, are not the evening destinations they used to be for a number of reasons ranging from safety, fewer two-parent homes, driving distances and inconvenience. The old tribe doesn't get together as much as it used to. But, if the authors are right, society is retribalizing on the Web and through mobile social networks.

How big is the problem—the P factor? It could involve more than 100 million people in the United States and two or three times that number in Europe and Asia. Cyworld, a South Korean start-up, has captured 30 percent of that country's population as members. At Cyworld, people create avatars, design their space with images that they download and pay for, receive and send videos from their place and conduct virtual business from their place—literally their third place.

One of the reasons that the Cyworld business model is so efficient is that it brings intense amounts of liquidity to a single community, thus making it less costly to introduce a myriad of revenue channels. For instance, the sale of objects with which MyThirdPlace.com (the name of this proposed U.S. version of CyWorld) members can design their places; affinity credit cards (e.g., Thirdplace Visa cards); tip jars to reward other members for excellence in storytelling shared with other members; kudo points for bringing in new members; revenues earned when a member forms an MLM sales organization to sell a community-approved product to other members, such as a life insurance policy; and subscription fees to first-run, major motion pictures. If MyThirdPlace.com grows to 30 million members quickly, and the community is unified, trusting and relatively free of defectors, it can negotiate volume discount deals on many consumer items from insurance to movies and from pharmaceuticals to apparel. It will have the power of the labor unions of the 1950s and 1960s, the Israeli kibbutzim of the same period and the soviets of the Soviet Union in the 1920s and 1930s.

MyThirdPlace.com's Raison d'Etre

You may ask what is the reason for being for MyThirdPlace.com. As Steinkuehler and Williams write, all of us need to have a place that we go to after work where they know our name.

Morpegs satisfy that need for about 12 million people in the United States, they wrote. I think the remainder of the population—those who do not play Morpegs—need the same rebalancing place. Think of the bar in *Cheers*. Think of Jerry's apartment or the coffee shop in *Seinfeld*. Think of the living room in *Friends* or Raymond's kitchen in *Everyone Loves Raymond*. Think of the bar at the golf club where your family were members, or the swimming pool where you splashed and laughed as a child. Think of all the places you have been outside your home or your office where you have shared worldviews and had a few good laughs.

If you can capture that ambience at MyThirdPlace.com, you could produce the greatest of all online communities. Your purchasing power will reshape all markets of consumer goods and services. And there will be so many strong revenue channels, MyThirdPlace.com will be advertising-free. Won't that be a unique model? The mob dictates the products and services they desire, the prices they will pay and the terms of purchase, delivery, after-delivery service and maintenance without advertising or salespeople.

25

IllegitimatiNonCarborundum.com

THE COMMUNITY that I have in mind for you now is one that serves *pro se* litigants. Sure, there are books and pamphlets on the subject, and law librarians are wonderful folks, but you can imagine how much more successful *pro se* litigants will become when knowledge is shared and the wisdom of crowds is tapped into.

We will call this community IllegitimatiNonCarborundum.com, or Illegitimati.com for short. The full phrase means "Don't let the bastards wear you down." (I am told by someone who was there that President Eisenhower had the phrase carved into a block of wood and it sat on his desk in the Oval Office.) I am inclined to recommend that this community serve civil complainants only, because criminal complainants lack money and frequently lack humor.

Let's assume that the IRS or your insurance carrier or a neighbor pisses you off to the point of fitful tirades and sleepless nights; but the cause of action is probably less than $30,000, and your lawyer would eat that up in a New York minute. So you don't want to hire him to sue the sumbitch; you're going to have to sue him yourself. What do you do next?

Seek Help at Illegitimati.com

You hear about Illegitimati.com by clicking through search engines and companies that amalgamate blogs. You visit the beautifully designed home page of the Illegitimati.com web portal and it makes you feel warm and cozy like the nave of a sixteenth-century Catholic church after you have paid for an indulgence. You're practically weeping with joy as you pay your $50 annual membership fee, enter your IP address and set forth a description of your anguish.

More than 30 *pro se* advisers write their solutions to you on the first day, including citations, Shepardized searches (with an explanation of Shepardizing) and assistance in writing the initial claim. On the second and third days even more help arrives, as 60 more *pro se* advisers provide their wisdom. Why so many helpers? Because Illegitimati's second revenue source is the tip jar. You reward the adviser who assisted you with a $500 to $3,500 tip. They hold on to 70 percent and the owners of Illegitimati keep 30 percent. Other readers of the advice forum may also give a tip to the best written advice, and that is divided up the same way.

Revenue Model

Let's assume that you are the founder of Illegitimati.com, and the field has no barriers to entry—anyone can copy your model—and every lawyer in the country, particularly those in the field of litigation, wants you shut down. You must operate quietly, confidently and professionally, with the highest standards in order to capture and hold the high ground. You cannot have attorneys in your ownership structure, as that would be off-putting to your clientele and could lead to ethics problems and conflicts of interest.

Let's assume that 500,000 lawsuits involve *pro se* litigants each year, and that you can lure 50,000 to your community. The lure will be done via SEO and viral marketing—influential bloggers spreading the word. Scanning the legal trade journals for lawsuits and mailing the poor buggers who were sued could bring in some customers as well. It could cost you several hundred thousand dollars to find 50,000 customers, and for that you may need $300,000 in seed capital. Some of that money could be used to buy servers and build the Web portal, create the forum pages, subscribe to LexisNexis and Westlaw and to print forms for motions, orders and the like.

However, Illegitimati.com should be the happy recipient of 5,000 member sign-ups a month at $50 a pop, producing revenues of $250,000 a month. These revenues can pay salaries and can be used to generate outreach marketing messages to *pro se* advisers who can give advice to the struggling pro se litigants.

As the sign-ups grow to perhaps 10,000 to 15,000 a month, revenues will grow to $500,000 to $750,000 a month. Most lawsuits take more than a year to resolve, and your customer base most likely will have to re-up for another year. Therefore, this is probably a recurring revenue model—the best kind—but not one with a long tail.

About halfway through year one, with say 45,000 *pro se* members signed up, the advisers will flock to the community and begin signing up as well in order to tap into tip-jar money. If the typical tip is $2,000 and if 60,000 *pro se* litigants each pay $2,000 in tips, the advisers will share a pool of 70 percent of $120 million, or $84 million. An adviser whose advice is selected 100 times will earn (using these numbers) $140,000. That's real money to a lot of people. It will definitely attract a crowd.

Illegitimati.com could generate tip-jar revenues of 30 percent of $120 million, or $36 million in year one. That should get any entrepreneur's juices flowing.

Keep It Jolly

Unlike travelers (www.PairingUp.com) or art buyers (www.ShareOurArt .com), the membership of Illegitimati will not be a jolly bunch of people.

They will be edgy and serious about righting a wrong. You could get sued by them for looking at them cross-eyed. Make sure the new members sign an agreement to mediate all disputes against your other members, member advisers and you and your fellow owners at the Metaverse Arbitration Association. (See Chapter 10.)

Also, you may want to give unexpected awards to the members to keep things light and lively. Show them some kindness to help take the edge off. The awards could be two tickets to Hawaii in consideration for the "excellence of your motion in *Jones v. IRS*" or something along those lines. And publish the news in the Illegitimati.com newsletter, so the recognition and the unexpected reward are known throughout the community.

Reputation Management

As I HAVE SAID, perhaps ad nauseum, online and mobile communities will live or die depending upon whether a user-demanded, user-orchestrated reputation management system is implemented that covers all users of all communities. The Internet is a public good, and online communities— the biggest wave to engulf the Internet since it began—are public goods. As Garrett Hardin warned us 40 years ago, it is in the nature of all of us to overgraze the commons with one extra cow. All mobile and online communities are at risk of suffering the tragedy of the commons unless they join hands, and unless their users interlock arms, and collectively fight to block out those people and organizations who will repeatedly and consistently and aggressively act in an uncooperative manner to their gain and to the detriment of others.

What's the Business Model?

The size of the problem, or P, is in the billions of dollars; in other words, if we, the users and community owners, don't self-regulate, then centralized authority in some unknown form, but probably something like the U.S. Homeland Security Department, will issue passes to use the Internet and mobile phones, and to pay for the new agency, we will be taxed.

The solution, or S, is a model that is similar to joining a national or international self-regulating off-line organization. There are hundreds of models to follow such as realtors, social workers, bar associations and the Association of Data Processing Service Organizations (ADAPSO), among others. Winemakers observe standards concerning the use of additives. Amateur basketball players in pick-up games observe self-imposed rules concerning fouls, out-of-bounds, length of game and skins versus shirts. In the online world, there is the nascent but highly serious group known as the Wikipedians, standard-setters for users of Wikipedia.com. An organization, perhaps an offshoot of the Association of Mobile and Online Communities, which I describe in Chapter 27, needs to be formed and funded. It needs user and owner representation in order to capture the concerns of all concerned.

The entrepreneurial team—the E factor—should be composed of men and women with regulatory experience and perhaps drawn from off-line associations where they distinguished themselves for their uprightness, probity, goodness and wisdom. Because the world of social networks is international, the regulatory body will have to be international as well.

The business model can be shaped along the lines of the United States Golf Association (USGA), which has a governing body, a rule book, a database of players and their handicaps, and it issues handicaps to the players. With a USGA card, an American can play St. Andrews, the legendary golf course in Fife, Scotland, where golf was invented. Or she can play at Bethpage, on Long Island in New York, with three other players whom the golfer has never met before. "Hello," she can say at the first tee as she shakes their hands, "I'm Sallie Smith, and I'm from Atlanta and my handicap is 12. Let's play a dollar Nassau." And when she says that, the other players know that her typical score is around 84 or 85 and that she would like to put a little skin into the game.

Translating that to the world of mobile and online communities, the person with the card issued by the reputation management association would be greeted by other members of the community as someone with a positive reputation who has been granted entry to the community by the universally regarded card-issuing organization.

What Freedoms Will Be Sacrificed?

Visitors to mobile and online communities will have to give up some freedoms. That's the sacrifice. That's the price to be paid in order to keep the "good" in *public good*. That's the price to be paid in order to avoid centralized authority. I envision communities requiring their members to join on a trial basis while their application for membership is uploaded to the reputation management organization. The word *trial* would appear next to their avatar or next to their IP address, or in their first text message in a mobile community. Other members, who have had their applications approved for membership, would see the word *trial* and be cautious of sharing too much information with that person until the word *trial* is eliminated.

If the word *trial* has not been eliminated for two weeks, the new member would be disqualified, and blocked with DRM software or its equivalent.

The Application Process

The governing body of the reputation management organization would develop a rule book not unlike that of the USGA, which has some wonderful sentences concerning penalties for grounding a club in a sand trap, striking a player's ball with your ball and plunking your ball into a body of water. The rules that are drawn up will be intended to block sex perverts and other psychopaths who attempt to hurt teenagers on sites designed for them, corporate flacks who pose as unattached individuals who attempt to promote their clients' products and services, and people who defect when the game they are playing or the auction they have entered requires cooperation—the kinds of people who are given low values on eBay.

Sure, people can register under multiple IP addresses and thus appear to be sheep, when they are in fact wolves in sheep's clothing. But through aggressive collaborative filtering, data mining, exchange of information between communities through the reputation management organization and pattern matching, people who change their online pseudonyms frequently can be discovered. ISP cooperation will be needed, but that should be relatively forthcoming.

Strategic Alliance with the Metaverse Arbitration Association

Repeat violators of the rules of the reputation management organization can be dealt with just as you and I are dealt with when we collect speeding tickets. We get brought before a tribunal with an opportunity to defend ourselves, in order to avoid losing our driver's license.

The reputation management organization merely notifies the MAA that a certain person, using the following pseudonyms and avatars on the following communities, is believed to be preying on children, or is not paying for goods purchased, or is not delivering the goods that he sold, or represents a certain Fortune 500 consumer products company and is posing as a 17-year-old who consumes that company's food products at every meal and believes that they eliminate the risk of heart attack.

The MAA can notify the person that a complaint has been filed against him, and he has 30 days to respond. He could hire an attorney from the panel described in Chapter 12 and defend himself. Or he could ignore it, and his card will be marked in the files of the reputation management organization, with a general announcement to ISPs and communities that a complaint has been filed against so-and-so and the person has elected not to defend himself; or he could defend himself and win, or defend himself and lose, in which case his card will be marked appropriately.

Retailers are sent a list of bad credit cards, and it seems to work. ISPs and communities that accept payment via credit cards and e-wallet cards can be notified by the reputation management organization that credit cards bearing the following numbers are deemed unacceptable by the reputation management organization.

Pulling the First Pickle Out of the Jar

It is not in the nature of entrepreneurs to stop their 120-mile-per-hour drive to grow, and to turn on a dime and come to a meeting concerning self-regulation. To get their attention, the organizers of the reputation management organization need to pick the first pickle out of the jar, and it should be the largest or one of the largest mobile or online communities. The representatives of the users could be selected from people who feel that their privacy has been invaded and who would like to see some brakes put on the cars racing around the Internet collecting members at lightning speed.

Facebook upset around 600,000 of its members back in September 2006, when information that should have been released to only a few close friends of a member was released to the membership at large. There was an outcry of protest from the Facebook members who felt their privacy had been violated. The more verbal of the Facebook members who felt invaded would possibly make good candidates to become cheerleaders for the new reputation management organization.

I was at the first meeting of ADAPSO. It was a dinner called by Senator Frank R. Lautenberg, who at the time was the vice president of marketing of Automatic Data Processing (ADP). He invited owners of keypunch operators and accounting services with names like Mail-Me-Monday, Inc., that did outsourced data processing on their IBM and Burroughs computers for businesses. Most of the data processors promised to get the finished work back to their clients in a week. FedEx had not been born yet, so the work was sent by couriers, trucks, and airline cargo operations. In a brilliant coup, Lautenberg had written each of the company's CEOs individually that he would like to meet them for dinner to discuss "areas of mutually beneficial interest." I suppose they thought that meant a possible acquisition, and that was certainly in the back of Lautenberg's mind. But he assembled about 25 CEOs at the meeting and, in addition to saying that ADP might like to buy them, he asked them to join him in forming the Association of Data Processing Service Organizations, or ADAPSO.

Is there a Frank Lautenberg out there with the brilliance and courage to launch a reputation management organization for mobile and online communities? If there is, now is your moment to take that one great step and leave your mark on perhaps the largest marketplace the planet has ever seen.

The Association of Mobile and Online Communities

THE BUSINESS OF THIS ONLINE COMMUNITY, which could be a dot-org in order to maintain the highest possible level of probity, is to be the standards- and policy-setting organization and one that charges fees from all of the online and mobile communities that believe in its validity.

Let's refer to it as Aomacom, and its web site is Aomacom.org. It will be based in or near Washington, D.C., of course, and it will have a well-paid staff whose functions will be to make sure no federal law is ever passed that could endanger online and mobile communities; to set policies and standards that mitigate the damage done by defectors, griefers and sexual predators; and to collect data from all online and mobile communities concerning membership, year-to-year changes in number of members, number of employees, year-to-year changes in employees, location of employees, average wage per employee and other census data.

The purpose of all of this is to be the positive voice of online and mobile communities when they are attacked from the pulpit, the press and the politician's podiums—as they surely will be. Whenever people are having too much fun and making too much money, they are definitely going to be attacked. It happened with the Whiskey Rebellion of 1790, the Salem witches, the rise of Lenny Bruce and profanity-laced comic acts, rock 'n' roll and file sharing, and it is going to happen with online and mobile communities. The best offense is a strong defense, and an association will be needed to speak for all online and mobile communities when the bricks start to fly.

Supported by Dues

The business model of Aomacom is quite simple. Each online and mobile community will pay annual dues according to their number of employees. If the range of dues is from $300 to $3,000 per year, with an average of $1,650, and if there are 10,000 online and mobile communities of which 8,000 sign up and pay dues, Aomacom will have $13.2 million in annual revenues. It will be able to hire 35 to 40 researchers and data gatherers and pay them $60,000 to $70,000 per annum. It will be able to publish reports, follow political murmurings concerning the industry, do some lobbying and press releasing when needed and create and maintain a positive image of online and mobile communities.

Strengthening Everyone's Business Model

Aomacom will host an annual convention at fabulous resorts that offer beaches, water sports, golf and tennis. The senior officers of all of the online and mobile communities will come to the annual event to participate in terrific seminars, play golf or other sports, hire away top executives from one another's companies and put together mergers and strategic alliances.

A handful of top-drawer journalists will be admitted—those who know and understand digital media and communities. The seminars will deal with everyone's favorite topics—how to make more money, increase stickiness, enhance liquidity and add revenue channels, and plans for taking over old media, spinning off their deadwood such as magazines and keeping their digital brands.

Booth space can be rented to service and appliance makers; lanyards and tote bag hand-outs can be paid for by sponsors; and caps, T-shirts and tchotchkes can be sold to attendees to add to revenues. See Chapter 12 for additional revenue-generating ideas.

Bibliography

Akst, Daniel. "Where Lender Meets Borrower, Directly." *New York Times*, February 5, 2006, 4.

Allison, Kevin. "The New Internet Independents." *Financial Times*, April 13, 2006, 13.

Angwin, Julia. "Parental Guidance." *Wall Street Journal*, July 24, 2006, 4–10.

Axelrod, Robert. *The Evolution of Cooperation*. New York: Basic Books, 1984.

Banya, Vinod, and John du Pre Gauntt. "The Gazillion-Dollar Question." *The Economist*, April 20, 2006.

Bartle, Dr. Richard A. "Pitfalls of Virtual Property." The Themis Group, April 2004. Accessed at www.themis-group.com/uploads/Pitfalls%20 of%20Virtual%20Property.pdf.

Batstone, David. "One-Stop Shopping to Save the World." *Business 2.0*, July 2006, 70.

Brown, Erika. "Game On!" *Forbes*, July 24, 2006, 84.

Buckman, Rebecca. "How Venture Capital Is Trying to Get Down with Young CEOs." *Wall Street Journal*, July 8–9, 2006, A12.

Butterworth, Trevor. "Blogged Off." *Financial Times*, February 19, 2006, 7–8; quoting Hugh Hewitt, writing in the *Weekly Standard* in August 2005.

Carr, Geoffrey. "The Story of Man." *Economist*, December 24, 2005.

Cassidy, John. "Me Media." *New Yorker*, May 15, 2006, 50–58.

Castronova, Edward. *Synthetic Worlds*. Chicago: University of Chicago Press, 2005, 121.

Chaplin, Heather, and Aaron Ruby. *Smartbomb: The Quest for Art, Entertainment, and Big Bucks in the Videogame Revolution*. Raleigh, NC: Algonquin Books, 2005.

Cialdini, Robert B. *Influence: The Psychology of Persuasion*. New York: William Morrow, 1993.

"Clip Culture." *Economist*, April 2, 2006, 68.

Darlin, Damon. "Goodbye Glue." *New York Times*, June 7, 2006, G1.

DeCesare, Chris. Speech at M-16 Conference, San Francisco, CA, July 16, 2006, Author's Notes.

Delaney, Kevin J. "With NBC Pact, YouTube Site Tries to Build a Lasting Business," *Wall Street Journal*, June 27, 2006, A1.

Dibbell, Julian. *Play Money, Or, How I Quit My Day Job and Made Millions Trading Virtual Loot*. New York: Basic Books, 2006, 22–25.

Eco, Umberto. *Foucault's Pendulum*. New York: Random House, 1988.

Edgecliffe-Johnson, Andrew. "MTV in Play for MySpace Generation." *Financial Times*, July 24, 2006, 15.

———. "Review Strikes a Sour Note as Merger Hopes Are Delayed." *Financial Times*, July 14, 2006, 14.

Elliott, Stuart. "Interpublic Is Moving Closer to a Big Consolidation." *New York Times*, April 28, 2006, C8.

Fass, Allison. "TheirSpace.com." *Forbes*, May 8, 2006, 122–124.

Fine, Jon. "A Billboard in Your Pocket." *BusinessWeek*, May 1, 2006, 26.

———. "Hide-and-Go-Seek an Ad." *BusinessWeek*, April 10, 2006, 22.

———. "Modern (Sigh) Media Maturity." *BusinessWeek*, December 12, 2005, 26.

"ForBiddeN Fruit." *Economist*, July 27, 2006, 60.

Fraser, Ian. "Viral Advertisers Play with Fire." *Financial Times*, August 29, 2006, 14.

Garfield, Bob. "Inside the New World of Listenomics: How the Open Source Revolution Impacts Your Brands." QwikFIND ID:AAR00T, October 11, 2005.

Giacobbe, Alyssa. "Spy Game." *TeenVogue*, September 2006, 138–142.

Green, Heather, and Robert G. Hof. "Your Attention Please." *Business-Week*, July 24, 2006, 48.

Grow, Brian. "Gold Rush." *BusinessWeek*, January 9, 2006, 69-76.

Hansell, Saul. "Making Friends Was Easy. Big Profit Is Tougher." *New York Times*, April 23, 2006, B1.

Hardin, Garrett. "The Tragedy of the Commons." *Science* (1968), accessed at http://dieoff.org/page95.htm.

Heilemann, John. "Branding the Feed." *Business 2.0*, July 2006, 42–44.

Hempel, Jessi. "A Little Money Goes a Long Way." *BusinessWeek*, July 31, 2006, 64.

Hof, Robert D. "Information Technology: New Media." *BusinessWeek*, July 24, 2006, 51.

———. "My Virtual Life." *BusinessWeek*, May 1, 2006, 72–80.

———. "Web 2.0: The New Guy at Work." *BusinessWeek*, July 19, 2006, 58.

Ibison, David. "Deal Could Be Music to Nokia's Ears." *Financial Times*, August 14, 2006, 14.

"In the Very Near Future." *Economist Technology Quarterly*, December 10, 2005.

Jacobson, David. "Hits and Misses." *Business 2.0*, July 2006, 132.

Jana, Reena. "On-the-Job Video Gaming." *BusinessWeek*, March 27, 2006, 43.

Kafka, Peter. "Blue Sky." *Forbes*, February 12, 2007, 86–92.

Kamenetz, Anya. "The Network Unbound." *Fast Company*, June 2006, 68.

Karlgaard, Rich. "Digital Rules." *Forbes*, August 14, 2006, 35.

Karnitschnig, Matthew. "Viacom Discovers Kids Don't Want Their MTV Online." *Wall Street Journal*, August 28, 2006, 1.

Khidekel, Marina. "Space Age." *CosmoGirl!*, August 2006, 104.

Kluth, Andreas. "Among the Audience." *Economist*, April 22, 2006, 3–18.

Koster, Raph. *A Theory of Fun for Game Design*. Scottsdale, AZ: Paraglyph Press, 2005.

Lacy, Sarah. "O Click All Ye Faithful." *BusinessWeek*, as reported on CNN.com, July 18, 2006.

Lacy, Sarah, and Jessi Hempel. "Valley Boys." *BusinessWeek*, August 14, 2006, 40–47.

"Lonely Nation." CNN.com, June 23, 2006, attributed to the Associated Press.

"The Long Arm of the Cell Phone", *Business Week*, November 6, 2006.

MacKenzie, Kate. "Advertisers Size Up Web 2.0." *Financial Times*, May 31, 2006, 36.

Malik, Om. "Putting the Customer in Charge." *Business 2.0*, July 12, 2006, 12.

———. "Sly Fox?" *Business 2.0*, July 2006, 101–105.

Marton, Kati. *The Great Escape: Nine Jews Who Fled Hitler and Changed the World*. New York: Simon & Schuster, 2006, 20.

Matail, Shlomo. *Economic Games People Play*. New York: Basic Books, 1984, 88, 112.

Matlack, Carol. "Young Spielbergs by the Thousands." *BusinessWeek*, December 19, 2005, 46.

Meacham, Jon. *Franklin and Winston: An Intimate Portrait of an Epic Friendship*. New York: Random House, 2003.

Meyer, Philip. *The Vanishing Newspaper: Saving Journalism in the Information Age*. Columbia, MO: University of Missouri Press, 2004.

Mullaney, Timothy J. "E-Tailers Try New Holiday Tricks." *BusinessWeek*, December 12, 2005.

———. "Lots of Loans." *BusinessWeek*, July 3, 2006, 72–73.

Murphy, Kate. "You've Opened the Gift. Now Give It a Review." *New York Times*, December 5, 2005, D4.

Murphy Barret, Victoria. "Googlespawn." *Forbes*, April 10, 2006, 50.

Nagourney, Adam. "Politics Is Facing Sweeping Changes via the Internet." *New York Times*, April 22, 2006, A1.

Nutall, Chris. "The Enriching Experience of Being an Avatar in a Metaverse." *Financial Times*, April 17, 2006, 14.

———. "When You Have Just 17 Minutes to Play With." *Financial Times*, May 24, 2006, 9.

Ohmae, Kenichi. *The Next Global Stage*. Philadelphia: Wharton School Publishing, 2005, 122, 225.

Pink, Daniel H. *A Whole New Mind*. New York: Riverhead Books, 2005, 79.

Project Tomorrow. NetDay 2005 Speak Up Event for Teachers and Students: Highlights from National Findings. Accessed at www .netday.org/SPEAKUP/.

Rheingold, Howard. *Smart Mobs*. New York: Perseus Books, 2002.

Ridley, Matt. *The Origins of Virtue*. New York: Penguin Group, 1996.

Rivlin, Gary. "Root, Root, Root for the Start-Up." *New York Times*, July 9, 2006, C1.

Safire, William. "On Language: Blargon." *New York Times Magazine*, February 19, 2006, 32.

Salinger, J. D. *Franny and Zooey*. New York: Little, Brown and Company, 1961, 1991.

Schiff, Stacy. "Know It All." *New Yorker*, July 31, 2006, 36.

Scoble, Robert, and Shel Israel. *Naked Conversations*. Hoboken, NJ: John Wiley & Sons, 2005, 5, 25.

Shaley, J. Lyndon, ed. *Walden. Economy*. Princeton, NJ: Princeton University Press, 1971, 23.

Shorto, Russell. *The Island in the Center of the World*. New York: Random House, 2002.

Silver, David. *Enterprising Women: Lessons from 100 of the Greatest Entrepreneurs of Our Day*. New York: Amacom, 1994.

Silverman, Gary. "How May I Help You?" *Financial Times*, February 5, 2006, W1.

Smith-Lovin, Lynn, Miller McPherson, and Matthew E. Brashears. "Social Isolation in America: Changes in Core Discussion Networks over Two Decades." *American Sociological Review* 71 (June 2006): 353–375.

Steinkuehler, Constance, and Dmitri Williams. "Where Everybody Knows Your (Screen) Name: Online Games as Third Places." *Journal of Computer-Mediated Communication* (August 2006). http://jcmc .indiana.edu/vol11/issue4/steinkuehler.html.

Sterling, Bruce. "Blogging for Dollars." *Wired*, June 2006, 126.

Surowiecki, John. *The Wisdom of Crowds*. New York: Doubleday, 2004.

"Technology Leads the Way as Online Learning Comes of Age." *Financial Times*, March 20, 2006.

Tocqueville, Alexis de. *Democracy in America*. New York: Penguin Putnam, 2003.

U.S. Census data at www.census.gov.

Van Duyn, Aline. "Whose Space? How Advertisers Are Struggling to Fathom Webwise Teens." *Financial Times*, May 24, 2006, 9.

Vara, Vauhini. "A Swap Meet for Your Used CDs." *Wall Street Journal*, April 28, 2006, D1.

Verini, James. "Will Success Spoil MySpace?" *Vanity Fair*, March 2006, 238-244.

Vollmer, Christopher, John Frelinghuysen, and Randall Rothenberg. "Waste in the Auto Advertising Media Mix," from "The Future of Advertising Is Now." *Strategy+Business*, August 15, 2006, 5. www .strategy-business.com/press/article/06204?pg=all.

Vranica, Susan. "Laughing All the Way to the Bank." *Wall Street Journal*, July 10, 2006, R1.

Wayner, Peter. "Site Tempts Video Makers by Offering to Pay Them." *New York Times*, July 3, 2006, C3.

"The Wiki Principle." *Economist*, April 22, 2006, 15.

Zeller, Tom, Jr. "A Generation Serves Notice." *New York Times*, January 22, 2006, B1.

Index